JAPAN

Managing Editor: Ruth Urbom

Project Editor: Christina Czapiewska

Jacket Design: Daniel Oliver

Design Layout: Daniel Oliver

Production and Editorial Manager: Karen Lomax

Authors: Ellen Flynn and Deborah Stowe

Metro Books
122 Fifth Avenue
New York, NY 10011

ISBN: 978-1-4351-1821-8

A catalog record for this title is available from the Library of Congress

Printed and bound in Malaysia

1 3 5 7 9 10 8 6 4 2

JAPAN

Secrets From The Land Of The Rising Sun

ELLEN FLYNN & DEBORAH STOWE

METRO BOOKS

NEW YORK

Contents

Land of Contrasts

Japan's geography is rich in contrasts: from dramatic mountains to serene gardens to ultra-modern cities, this island nation offers a fascinating range of environments.

Japan has long held a special fascination for Westerners. For many centuries, the feudal lords who ruled over Japan maintained a strict policy of isolation. This lack of contact with other nations meant that Japan developed its own unique and very distinct language and culture. With such a degree of difference between Japanese ways and our own, it may seem like an impossible task to get to know Japan really well. This book aims to give a few intriguing insights into the land, its people, their culture and customs.

Somehow, Japan always seems to be one step ahead of the rest of the world, with its endless stream of hi-tech gadgets and equipment, futuristic super-fast trains, and gleaming modern skyscrapers. Yet at the same time, Japan remains firmly rooted in its past, with strong ties to its history and traditions woven into the structure of its culture and society.

The islands that make up present-day Japan have been inhabited by people since prehistoric times. Scientists do not agree about exactly when the first humans traveled to the Japanese archipelago, but there is certainly evidence of hunter-gatherers in the Late Palaeolithic period over 25,000 years ago. New waves of settlers migrated from the Korean peninsula between 500 BC and 500 AD. These people subsisted on fishing and rice agriculture—still two staples of the Japanese diet in the 21st century.

The dozens of "countries" which existed on the Japanese archipelago in the early centuries AD began to amalgamate into what could be termed a nation-state, with the development of administrative systems assisted by the spread of writing, from the 5th century AD.

Today, Japan is a democratic nation with a population of over 125 million. Its total land area is a little less than that of the state of California, but much of the interior is too mountainous to be developed. Because of this, the coastal regions are very densely populated and living space is at a premium. This means that buildings have often had to go upwards rather than outwards, so many people in Japan live in high-rise apartment buildings.

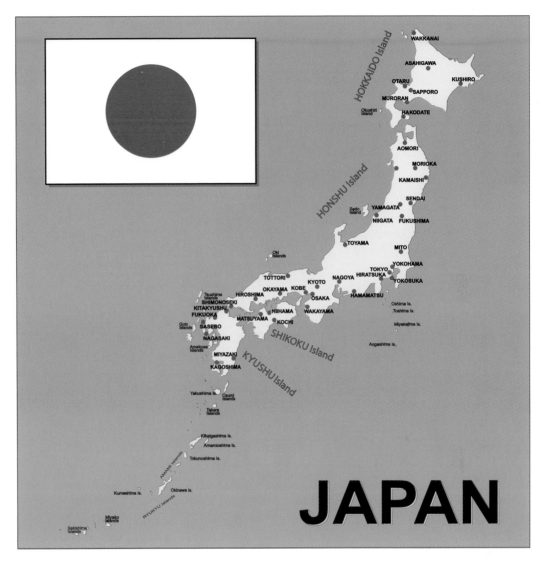

JAPAN

Japan always seems to be one step ahead of the rest of the world, with its endless stream of hi-tech gadgets and equipment, futuristic super-fast trains, and gleaming modern skyscrapers.

Above: Japan's island geography has had a significant influence on its history and culture.

Left: Modern business attire and the traditional kimono: just one of the contrasts of today's Japan.

Above: Space is at a premium in Japanese cities.

Stretching out at the southernmost end of the Japanese archipelago are a number of small islands which enjoy a subtropical climate. These places are enjoyed by many Japanese residents of the larger main islands as vacation destinations, but their remoteness from the centers of business and industry limit their economic prospects.

And Japan's location at the edge of the Pacific Ocean and on several tectonic fault lines means that its residents experience Mother Nature's wrath in many different ways: typhoons, earthquakes, and volcanoes. The people of Japan have learned to cope with these forces, though, and have developed building methods that are highly resistant to earthquakes and other natural disasters.

The familiar image of the Japanese national flag, featuring its simple, iconic motif of a red disc centered on a plain white background, is emblematic of its position off the eastern edge of the Eurasian landmass. The red disc symbolizes the early-morning sun. Indeed, *Nihon*, the name for the country in the Japanese language, actually means "land of the rising sun."

Legend has it that flags with the same basic design of a red disc on a white background have been used as symbols of Japan since the 13th century. It is said that a Buddhist priest gave such a flag to the Japanese emperor, who was considered to be a direct descendant of the sun goddess Amaterasu.

While this flag, known as the *nisshoki* or "sun flag" was in common use on Japanese ships by the second half of the 19th century, it was actually not until 1999 that a government proclamation signaled its official adoption as the national flag.

Modern-day Japan is divided up into 47 districts, called prefectures, for government and administrative purposes. Prefectural governments have some control over local matters such as education and environmental issues. The national parliament of Japan is called the Diet, or *kokkai* in Japanese. The Diet consists of two legislative houses. The head of Japan's national government is the prime minister. But a strong link with Japan's long history remains in the form of the Japanese emperor

Because Japan covers quite a range of latitudes from north to south, it has quite a variety of climates. The island of Hokkaido in the north is actually not that far from eastern Siberia, so it has winters with plenty of snow. Much of Hokkaido is mountainous, including many craters of extinct volcanoes, but there are also areas of gently rolling plains which are rare in the rest of Japan.

Warm ocean currents passing along the eastern coastlines of Japan help to make the winters somewhat milder on Honshu, the main central island. Cities such as Tokyo can be sweltering in the summertime. This is not that surprising when you consider that Tokyo is actually on a similar latitude to the Mediterranean coast of North Africa and Virginia in the United States.

and the rest of the imperial family. Although the emperor no longer wields any real political power under the modern Japanese Constitution, he still enjoys great respect from the people of Japan. Members of the imperial household live in isolation from the rest of the population, and they observe very formal rules of etiquette and protocol which have remained in place for centuries.

Members of the Japanese imperial family have their own flags, which feature a stylized picture of a chrysanthemum flower in the center. The chrysanthemum is the symbol of the imperial family, and the position of the emperor is officially known as the Chrysanthemum Throne.

Past and present, tradition and innovation—these qualities are ever-present in today's Japan. Let's begin our exploration in the exciting metropolis that is the nation's economic powerhouse.

Below: A bustling street scene.

Tokyo

Tokyo is truly a city of superlatives. Not only is it Japan's largest city and the seat of its government and the imperial family, it ranks as one of the world's mega-cities. Over 8 million people live in the city of Tokyo proper, but if you include all of the greater metropolitan Tokyo area, the population is a whopping 35 million—that's more than the population of many countries around the world.

But the origins of this now-huge urban center were extremely modest, and there were many setbacks during its earliest years, with hardly any indication of the greatness that was to come in later centuries.

The original settlement that would come to be known as Tokyo was, in fact, established as a small fishing village in the 7th century AD. The village was known as Edo from the late 12th century onwards.

In 1603, Edo became Japan's political center when Tokugawa Ieyasu, a warrior leader known as a *shogun*, founded a dynasty that was to rule over Japan for some 300 years. Through a series of battles, Tokugawa Ieyasu defeated other warrior chieftains to consolidate his power and establish a form of government that was preserved by force. Tokugawa Ieyasu chose Edo to be the seat of his government. At this time, however, the true capital was still located in Kyoto, farther to the southwest of Edo, because that was where the emperor and his court officially resided and had already done so for over a thousand years.

A wooden castle, now referred to as Edo Castle, was built in the 1630s. By the mid-17th century, Edo had grown into a major city by the standards of that time. It was an important commercial center as a result of the concerted policy of urbanization instituted by Tokugawa Ieyasu. Merchants and craftsmen, tea sellers, medicine peddlers, and brothel-keepers all came to the city to provide the amenities needed by the elite *samurai* warrior class. With the economic activity brought about by urbanization came a new class of patrons of literature and the arts. Literacy spread

through the population during the Tokugawa period, and a new industry of woodblock printing boomed to meet the public's hunger for books of all kinds.

In 1657, though, a great fire swept through Edo, destroying the castle and killing over 100,000 people. Many of the houses were flimsy and poorly constructed of wood, and certainly very tightly packed together, which meant that fire could spread rapidly. The fire burned for 19 days before it could be put out completely.

Then in 1707, Mount Fuji—that familiar Japanese landmark, which is actually a volcano—erupted and covered Edo in volcanic ash. Edo suffered yet another disaster in 1855, when it was hit by a powerful earthquake.

By the mid-19th century, the ruling *shogun* was coming under pressure from many sides: increasing tensions between urban rich and poor erupted into violence and riots; inflation was causing economic instability; ocean vessels from foreign nations were making ever stronger attempts to gain contact with Japan, bringing a threat of war.

Finally, in 1867, Tokugawa Yoshinobu, the last *shogun* ruler, realized that he no longer had sufficient power to resist these dangers, and surrendered his power to the emperor's military forces. In 1868 the *shogun* fled Edo and the rule shifted to representatives of the emperor. The emperor himself assumed power in 1869 and moved to Edo, taking up residence in the castle there, which then became the imperial castle. The emperor changed the city's name from Edo to Tokyo, meaning "eastern capital." With the transfer of the emperor and his government from Kyoto, Tokyo became the new capital of Japan. However, because this was actually only a de facto change which was never formally enshrined in law, there are some people who maintain that Kyoto is still the official capital, or at least the co-capital, of Japan.

The period of Japanese history that lasted from the transfer of power to the emperor in 1868 until 1912 is known as the Meiji period, after the emperor himself. Similarly, the transfer of power is referred to as the Meiji Restoration. Actually, the emperor's name was Mutsuhito, but after his death he was assigned a descriptive name, in accordance with imperial custom. *Meiji* actually means "enlightened rule," and today the Meiji period is commonly regarded as a time of progress and new openness to the rest of the world. This is an oversimplification, but it can nevertheless be said that the changes that were started during this time laid the groundwork for Japan's rise to its position of pre-eminence in the world of today. Japanese people are proud of this period of their country's history.

Above: The daily rush of commuters.

Left: Japanese cities offer an overwhelming array of colors and images.

Above: The city at sunset:
there's still plenty of activity.

In September 1923, Tokyo was hit by a severe earthquake. Over 100,000 people lost their lives, and many homes and buildings were destroyed. The scale of destruction was made even worse by the time the quake struck: it was lunchtime, when many people were preparing meals using fire. Flames spread rapidly through the city and were fanned by winds from a typhoon. Many people perished in firestorms following the actual earthquake. In the aftermath of the disaster, some officials considered moving the capital elsewhere. Instead, Tokyo was rebuilt with improved safety measures such as parks and open spaces to which people could retreat in case of another earthquake. Because of the memory of the huge scale of destruction, schools and other organizations in Tokyo regularly hold disaster drills. New construction projects in Tokyo must comply with strict building regulations for the sake of safety.

Today, visitors to Tokyo will experience a full-on sensory overload from this fast-paced city. The city is divided into 23 districts known as "special wards," each of which has its own name and identity. Some areas are mainly residential, while others are dominated by office buildings or other types of establishments.

Shinjuku is home to the Tokyo metropolitan government as well as many of the city's earliest skyscrapers, dating from the 1970s. Shinjuku station is the world's busiest train and subway station. Over 3 million people pass through this major transportation hub every day!

Ginza is a famous upscale shopping district with many department stores, restaurants, and art galleries. Land in Ginza commands prices upwards of 10 million yen (roughly $100,000) per square *meter*, which makes it some of the priciest in all of Japan. Ginza is a popular place to go for a stroll on weekends, because the main north-south street is closed to traffic then, making it a pleasant place to spend a leisurely afternoon.

*Right: Sleek modern
Tokyo style.*

*Below right: A vibrant
nighttime scene.*

Younger visitors might find the districts of Harajuku and Shibuya more to their liking. Harajuku is the place where Tokyo's trendiest teenagers go to see and be seen. And they don't just turn up in plain jeans and T-shirts: Harajuku is the place to make a fashion statement. All sorts of outlandish youth trends get their start in Harajuku. Such is the fast-moving nature of youth fashion that by the time someone manages to write about the hottest craze, the trendsetters have already abandoned it and moved on to something else. Nevertheless, two noteworthy youth styles of the first decade of the 21st century have achieved global attention among the fashion cognoscenti. "Gothic Lolita" is a look adopted by some teenage girls that involves frilly little-girl-style dresses trimmed with lace, but with a decidedly grown-up twist. Black is a popular color choice (hence the "Gothic" in the name). Other young women choose to go for the look known as *ganguro*, which draws its inspiration from suntanned California beach babes, but then takes it in a completely different direction. Ganguro girls have bleached blonde hair and fake tans, set off by exaggerated white eye shadow and lipstick. Their clothes and cheap plastic jewelry display a riot of bright, '80s-style colors.

Shibuya, located close to Harajuku, has plenty of nightclubs, as well as numerous fashion department stores. It, too, has a busy train and subway station. A well-known landmark just outside Shibuya station is a bronze statue commemorating an Akita dog named Hachiko, who lived in the 1920s and '30s. Every day Hachiko would sit near the exit from Shibuya station, waiting for his master, a university professor, to return from work and so the dog became a familiar sight there. The story is all the more poignant because Hachiko's owner died in 1925, but the dog continued to return faithfully to the station each day to wait for his master until his own death in 1935. Hachiko became famed throughout Japan for his loyalty and obedience—qualities that are highly valued in Japanese society. Today, the Hachiko statue is a popular place for friends to arrange to meet up before heading off to do some shopping or sightseeing together.

Tokyo is full of unusual and unexpected sights for the visitor. But there are many other cities and regions in Japan to discover, each with its own history and charm.

Yokohama

Though Yokohama is a major city in its own right, over the years it has become swallowed up by the ever-increasing urban development of greater Tokyo. Many residents of Yokohama commute to work in Tokyo daily. The distance is only 18 miles (30 km), and the frequent high-speed bullet trains that zip between the two urban centers can handle a large number of commuters each day. Yokohama is also well connected to other cities in Japan via a number of other rail lines.

Located on the western rim of Tokyo Bay on Japan's main island of Honshu, Yokohama began as a small fishing village but rose to prominence as an important port city after the Meiji Restoration of 1868 opened Japan to trade with the rest of the world. One result of Yokohama's long-time contact with foreign influences is its Chinatown district, which is the largest in

Japan. Early trading focused on silks and craft items such as porcelain and lacquerware. In the late 19th century, Japan participated in many international exhibitions and world fairs around the globe. These events helped to create interest in Japan and its culture and products. The interest was reciprocal: people in the port city of Yokohama and elsewhere in Japan welcomed input and development from other nations. As a result, many foreign influences first took hold in Yokohama before going on to become established in the rest of Japan. The first daily newspaper began to be published in Yokohama in 1870. Two years later, Japan's first railway line started running a passenger service between Yokohama and Tokyo, and the nation's first coal-fired power plant started generating electricity.

Yokohama experienced rapid industrial growth in the early 20th century, and many people in the

Below left: Yokohama is an important port city.

Below right: The Landmark Tower in Yokohama is the tallest building in Japan.

city became very wealthy. Large parts of Yokohama and Tokyo were destroyed in an earthquake in 1923, and further damage and loss of life occurred in bombing raids during World War II. Today, Yokohama has modern urban developments centered around the harbor area and on reclaimed land, as well as large industrial areas along the coastline and suburban residential developments to the north of the city center.

In 2002, the final championship game in the soccer World Cup was played between Germany and Brazil in Yokohama's International Stadium. Yokohama may be overshadowed in many ways by Tokyo, its larger neighbor, but it does boast the largest building in all of Japan on its Waterfront Parade in the ultramodern Minato Mirai 21 district. The Landmark Tower stands some 970 feet (295 m) tall and contains a hotel on its upper floors, with offices and retail spaces on its lower floors. It will retain its status as Japan's tallest habitable building beyond 2011, when a huge new broadcasting tower called Sumida Tower is expected to be completed in Tokyo. At an estimated 2,000 feet (613.5 m) in height, the planned tower will be the tallest free-standing structure not only in Japan, but in the entire world. Once again, Japan is proving its technological expertise and forward-looking attitude.

Above: Yokohama is located on Tokyo Bay.

Mount Fuji

Known to Japanese speakers as *Fuji-san*, Mount Fuji is the highest peak in Japan at 12,388 feet (3,776 m). Its distinctive shape, almost a perfect cone, has become a well-known symbol of Japan through numerous depictions in artwork, literature, and photography—in fact, enthusiasts of the Japanese craft of *origami* have even developed folded paper models of the majestic mountain, complete with its contrasting cap of snow. In past centuries, Mount Fuji was worshipped as a sacred site. Many famous Japanese and foreign painters have chosen Mount Fuji as a subject, and it also makes frequent appearances in Japanese poetry. Another, more surprising, stylized representation of Mount Fuji's symmetrical shape can be seen in the logo of the Atari videogame company.

Towering majestically above the surrounding landscape, Mount Fuji is visible on a clear day from Tokyo, approximately 60 miles (100 km) away. Due to increasing pollution, such clear days have become less frequent than in past centuries, though recent efforts to improve air quality have helped improve the situation.

Although much of Japan is mountainous, Mount Fuji is special because it is actually a volcano. Fortunately for the people who live in the vicinity, Mount Fuji has not erupted since 1707. Scientists say that there is currently a very low risk of another eruption. The ash-based soil around Mount Fuji is not particularly fertile because it is poor in nutrients.

Mount Fuji is surrounded by five lakes: Lake Kawaguchi, Lake Yamanaka, Lake Sai, Lake Motosu, and Lake Shoji. It is located within a national park, the Fuji-Hakone-Izu National Park. Tourists can enjoy a visit to Hakone, a natural hot springs resort in the region. There is also a forest at the base of Mount Fuji. Aokigahara Forest, which is also known as *Jukai*, or the "sea of trees," is associated with many legends

of monsters and ghosts. Perhaps one reason for the large number of spooky stories is the high level of magnetized iron content in the forest soil, which causes magnetic compasses to behave irregularly. There are also icy caverns dotted throughout Aokigahara Forest. The forest is also very dense and eerily silent in its depths, except when the wind rustles through the leaves of the trees.

Mount Fuji is actually a volcano. Fortunately for the people who live nearby, Mount Fuji has not erupted since 1707.

Above: The majesty of Mount Fuji.

Left: Mount Fuji and cherry blossoms: two symbols of Japan.

Left: A traditional torii, *or gate, near Mount Fuji.*

Below: Mount Fuji is surrounded by five lakes.

Right: A carefully maintained tea plantation near Mount Fuji.

The first foreigner to climb to the top of Mount Fuji was Sir Rutherford Alcock, a British diplomat, in 1860. Nowadays trails are open to climbers during the months of July and August so everyone can climb right to the top of Mount Fuji. There are mountain huts along the way with restaurants and rooms for overnight stays. Climbers are advised to wear sturdy footwear and take a flashlight for nighttime climbing, as well as sufficient food and water, especially for the trails that have fewer mountain huts where food can be purchased along the way. The peak is generally free from snow during the summer. Climbing Mount Fuji is such a popular activity during the August vacation season with Japanese and foreign tourists alike that there are sometimes bottlenecks at certain points along the hiking trails. But with the right attitude, being among hundreds of like-minded climbers can create a great feeling of camaraderie. Many climbers time their ascents so as to be able to enjoy the spectacular sunrise from high up on the mountain. Guided hiking tours are also available for those who do not wish to tackle the climb on their own. Once at the top, successful hikers can complete a circuit around the edge of the volcanic crater, which takes about an hour. Japan's highest point is located along the rim of the crater.

Some more daring types take mountain bikes along. It takes a brave rider to attempt the descent on a bike, though, and it can be very risky when there are many people on foot along the path.

There are plenty of other activities that people enjoy in the vicinity of Mount Fuji, including paragliding. The smaller hills nearby serve as convenient takeoff and landing places.

Mount Fuji also has connections to warriors that stretch far back in history. Ancient samurai warriors used to train near the base of the mountain. Their training activities included a special type of archery performed on horseback. Nowadays, the Japanese military has a modern base near Mount Fuji. Training exercises are often held in the dense Aokigahara Forest nearby.

The mythical creature, *Shachihoko*, was thought to cause rain; symbols of *Shachihoko* were often placed on top of wooden buildings to protect them from fire.

Left: Mount Fuji stands distinct from the Yatsugatake mountain range.

Below: The ancient Nagoya castle.

Nagoya

Nagoya is Japan's fourth largest city. It is a major port city and industrial center, located on a coastal inlet on eastern Honshu between the huge metropolitan areas of Tokyo-Yokohama and Kobe-Kyoto-Osaka. Important industrial products in Nagoya's history include pottery, cotton, and gunpowder.

Part of Nagoya's port district has been redeveloped into a leisure and shopping area, including an aquarium and museums. Visitors can also travel outside the city to take a tour of a Toyota car factory. The car manufacturer's global headquarters and factory tours are located in the city of Toyota, which is about an hour east of Nagoya, but it is also possible to gain some insights into this major corporation in Nagoya itself by paying a visit to the Toyota Techno Museum.

Perhaps Nagoya's most important tourist destination is Nagoya Castle, which was originally constructed in 1612. The castle suffered significant damage in World War II and was later restored in the 1950s. Its traditional exterior conceals one very modern feature in its restored interior—an elevator. The most significant parts of the castle's outward appearance are the two golden *shachihoko* on the roof. *Shachihoko* are mythical creatures with the head of a tiger and the body of a carp. In ancient times, people believed that these creatures could cause rain to fall, so figures of them were often placed on top of wooden buildings as symbolic protection from fire.

Younger visitors to Nagoya might be more interested in visiting its Pokemon theme park, centered around the popular cartoon character and his colorful friends.

Kyoto

Kyoto was Japan's capital city and the emperor's residence from 794 until the Meiji Restoration of 1868, when the emperor relocated the capital from Kyoto to Tokyo. It is now the country's seventh-largest city with a population of 1.4 million and is part of the large metropolitan area also comprising the cities of Osaka and Kobe. Kyoto's historical and cultural significance is perhaps unrivaled in Japan.

In the year 794, the Emperor Kanmu established the seat of his power in the city of Heian-kyo, meaning "capital of peace and tranquility." This city lent its name to the Heian period of Japanese history, which lasted from 794 to 1185.

This period represented the height of Japanese feudal culture and private land ownership. At this time, the emperor was more of a spiritual and cultural leader with little political power. The real power and authority was wielded by the *shogun*, or military dictators. By the 12th century, the ruling warrior class of samurai under the *shogun* had consolidated their power to such an extent that they had a great deal of leisure time. They began to focus on cultural pursuits such as Zen Buddhism. Martial arts were also popular. Japanese classical art forms such as painting, calligraphy, and literature blossomed in the imperial court during the Heian era and beyond under the rule of the *shogun*.

Below: A place for quiet contemplation.

*Above: Kyoto boasts over 2,000
temples and shrines.*

Kyoto was Japan's capital city from 794 until 1868, when the emperor relocated the capital from Kyoto to Tokyo.

Left: Visitors to ancient Kyoto can choose this interesting form of transportation.

Below: Kinkaku-ji, the Temple of the Golden Pavilion in Kyoto.

One member of the imperial court in the Heian era was a lady-in-waiting known as Murasaki Shikibu. She is remembered today for her significant contribution to Japanese literature. Murasaki, or Lady Murasaki as she is often known in English, was born in Kyoto around the year 978. Her real name is not known; Murasaki was a nickname given to her, meaning "purple wisteria blossom," and Shikibu refers to the rank or occupation of her father. Murasaki wrote poetry and a diary, but her most important work is known as the *Tale of Genji* ("Genji Monogatari" in Japanese). This latter work is considered by many scholars to be the world's very first novel, though there is still some debate in academic circles about whether it is really properly called a novel. Aspects that make it characteristic of a novel include several main characters and numerous subsidiary characters—in fact, the work contains over 400 characters in all—as well as a sequence of events that occur in the characters' lives. The *Tale of Genji* tells of the life of a son of a Japanese emperor, with particular emphasis on his romantic life. It gives readers many useful insights into life in the aristocratic class of the time.

Today, a scene from the *Tale of Genji* is performed by actors in historical costumes every year in Kyoto as part of the city's springtime *Aoi Matsuri* festival, which also features performances of martial arts and other activities from the Heian era. The story has also been made into films (both live action and animated) as well as an opera.

The feudal capital city of Heian-kyo was eventually renamed Kyoto. The syllable *kyo*, as found in some Japanese city names such as Kyoto and Tokyo, means "capital city." While English speakers generally pronounce Kyoto with three syllables, the Japanese pronunciation has only two syllables, each with a lengthened "oh" sound at the end: "kyoh-toe."

Over the centuries, Kyoto suffered destruction and damage by many wars and fires, but it was spared from air raids during World War II because of its important historic value. As a result, Kyoto is home to over 2,000 temples and shrines and many other important historical structures today. Experts and laypeople the world over say that Kyoto's architectural heritage is unsurpassed in Japan. Its skyline features an impressive mix of historic buildings and temples as well as sleek modern buildings. Streets in the central parts of the city, both ancient and modern, are laid out in a grid pattern.

Kyoto is surrounded by mountains on three sides. This creates a climate with hot summers and cold winters.

Kyoto Gosho, the Kyoto imperial palace, was the official residence of Japan's imperial family until the emperor relocated his seat of power to Tokyo. The palace is located in the Kyoto Imperial Park. The present palace dates from 1855. Earlier versions of the imperial palace burned down or were moved around the city several times through the centuries. The palace complex consists of many gates, halls, and formal gardens, and the grounds are enclosed by a long wall. The Kyoto imperial palace can be visited only on guided tours, which must be specially arranged in advance.

Above: Festive lanterns decorate this torii, *or temple gate.*

Right: Space is at a premium in this Kyoto cemetery.

Kinkaku-ji ("Temple of the Golden Pavilion") is a Zen temple set in breathtaking landscaped grounds in Kyoto. Its formal name is Rokuon-ji, meaning "deer garden temple," but its more popular name refers to its opulent exterior covering of pure gold leaf. Construction started on the Golden Pavilion in 1397 as part of a new residence for the retired *shogun* Ashikaga Yoshimitsu. After Yoshimitsu's death in 1408, his son converted Kinkaku-ji into a Zen temple. The temple complex was said to evoke paradise on earth. The Golden Pavilion houses sacred relics of the Buddha. The present building dates from 1955 because the original pavilion was burned down by a mentally disturbed monk in 1950.

Its exterior was restored in the 1980s with a thicker protective covering of lacquer over the gold leaf.

Yoshimitsu's grandson constructed another Buddhist temple in Kyoto, now known as Ginkaku-ji, which drew its inspiration from Kinkaku-ji. It was originally intended that Ginkaku-ji would be covered in silver leaf, as a counterpart to the earlier golden temple. However, due to the straitened economic circumstances brought about by a war that was being fought at the time, the exterior of the temple was left uncovered. Today it is regarded as a prime example of Japanese aesthetic restraint.

Left: A geisha entering a traditional teahouse in Kyoto.

Kyoto's architectural heritage is unsurpassed in Japan; the area is home to over 2,000 temples, shrines, and many other important historical structures.

To-ji is another important temple in Kyoto. Its name means "eastern temple," and it is well-known in Japan for its five-story pagoda, which is the tallest in the country, standing some 188 feet (57 m) tall. To-ji was founded in the year 794, the same year in which Kyoto achieved its status as Japan's new capital city. It originally stood near another temple, called Saiji, or "western temple," alongside the *Rashomon*, or entrance gate to the Heian capital. The impressive Buddhist sculptures on display in the temple's large halls are also justly famous. To-ji is one of many UNESCO World Heritage Sites in and around Kyoto. Visitors to To-ji may choose to pay a visit to a monthly flea market that is held in the grounds around To-ji.

Today, Kyoto's economy is based to a large extent on tourism. Industry has a less significant presence here, though some well-known global names in the field of electronics have their headquarters in Kyoto—most notably the computer game maker Nintendo, as well as electronic equipment manufacturers Kyocera and Murata Machinery. Japan's film and TV industry has an important

presence in Kyoto. Many samurai action movies were shot on sets at the Toei Uzumasa Eigamura studio. Sometimes filming for movies or television programs is done in the city of Kyoto itself, and people can watch the action as it happens.

Kyoto is also an important academic center in Japan. Thirty-seven colleges and universities are located here, including the prestigious Doshisha and Kyoto universities, which are considered among the best in Japan. Kyoto University counts several Nobel laureates among its faculty members.

Above: The Minamizu kabuki theater in Kyoto.

Left: A stone sculpture in Kyoto.

Osaka

Osaka is often referred to as Japan's "second city." It actually ranks third in the nation in terms of population behind Tokyo and Yokohama, but Osaka is part of a major metropolitan area including the cities of Kyoto and Kobe. Osaka is an important commercial center, and many people commute into the city to work each day—so many, in fact, that the city's daytime population is approximately 40 percent larger than its nighttime population, which is a greater ratio than in any other Japanese city.

Osaka was formerly known as Naniwa. In the early centuries of the Japanese imperial succession, the custom was for each new emperor to move his capital to a new location. In 645 AD, Emperor Kotoku established his palace in the area that now includes Osaka. It was then called Naniwa-kyo. The city maintained its status as capital for ten years until Kotoku's death. It was made capital once again in 744, but the imperial court moved to Heijyo-kyo (now known as the city of Nara) the next year.

Natives of Osaka have long had a reputation for being energetic, outgoing, and good at business, and Osaka quickly grew into a major commercial center. The city is located on the edge of Osaka Bay and is surrounded by other smaller cities on its other sides. In recent years, some large corporations have moved their headquarters from Osaka to Tokyo, and as a result the city's mayor has spearheaded a campaign to attract more national and international investment into Osaka.

One of Japan's most famous castles is Osaka Castle. The castle building that is standing today is a concrete reproduction of the original. The modern version was begun in 1931, with the latest renovation work completed in 1997. Its interior is completely different in appearance from the original wooden castle, though. The original castle was built in 1583 by a feudal ruler who wanted to create a formidable edifice that would repel attackers and surpass other castles in its grandeur, with gold leaf trim to impress visitors. He intended it to become the center of a new, unified Japan.

Unfortunately for his successor, though, the castle was attacked and destroyed in 1615. It was soon rebuilt, but was struck by lightning and burned down in 1665. After that, the castle fell into neglect for some time. Today, the modern version of the castle houses a museum that tells of the history of Osaka Castle.

Another significant place in Osaka is the Shintenoji Temple. Originally built in 593 AD, this is the oldest Buddhist temple in Japan. It was constructed by Prince Shotoku, who wished to encourage the spread of Buddhism. The temple's tower is a five-story pagoda which has been rebuilt since its original construction.

Even older is the Sumiyoshi Taisha, one of Japan's oldest Shinto shrines. It was founded in the 3rd century AD. Sumiyoshi Taisha is mentioned as a location in the *Tale of Genji*, the great work of classical Japanese literature. The shrine's indigenous Japanese style of architecture predates Buddhist temple styles, which were imported from China. The Sumiyoshi Taisha shrine is located in northern Osaka.

Left: Some of Osaka's gleaming modern skyscrapers.

Right: Like other Japanese cities, Osaka also has many traditional buildings, such as the Shintenoji Temple pagoda.

Over: Reflections of modern Osaka.

Left: Osaka Castle was built on a tall stone platform for protection from attack.

Right: A monument in Osaka to commemorate the end of war.

Osaka is particularly well known throughout Japan for its cuisine. A favorite saying in Osaka translates as, "Dress 'til you drop in Kyoto; eat 'til you drop in Osaka"—meaning that fashion devotees who have been shopping for new clothes in the fashionable stores of Kyoto may have to loosen the tie belts of their traditional *kimono* when they come to sample the regional specialties of Osaka. The city has its own special types of sushi and noodle dishes, as well as more exotic treats like octopus dumplings.

Another special feature of Osaka's cultural life is the *bunraku* puppet theater. This is a very special, traditional Japanese art form with a long history. The National Bunraku Theater in Osaka is one of the few places where people can view this unique form of entertainment. Unusually, *bunraku* was always intended to be enjoyed by ordinary people rather than members of the nobility. In this regard, *bunraku* is similar to *kabuki*, another traditional Japanese theater style.

The dialect of Japanese spoken by Osakans is known throughout Japan for its distinctive characteristics which mark it out from the standard language. *Osaka-ben*, as the dialect is called in Japanese, is often described as more melodic in tone and also somewhat harsher than standard Japanese. Many standard Japanese words are typically shortened in *Osaka-ben*, and in some cases entirely different words are used to refer to the same thing or idea. As a result, some expressions used by Osakans can sound very strange to Tokyo residents.

Kobe and Himeji

Many Westerners may have first become aware of the city of Kobe in early 1995, when the city was devastated by a massive earthquake. The quake struck early one morning in January and measured 7.3 on the Richter scale. Over 5,000 people lost their lives in that natural disaster, many tens of thousands were injured, and thousands of buildings were destroyed.

Today, however, Kobe has been completely rebuilt and little evidence of the destruction remains visible. Kobe is one of the ten largest cities in Japan, and its location on the coast west-southwest of Osaka and Kyoto means that it is an important port city and commercial center. Kobe was one of the first ports in Japan to open to foreign trade in the Meiji period of Japanese history, which started in 1868. As a result of its early contact with the outside world, Kobe has long been considered one of Japan's most cosmopolitan cities. Today it has a relatively large population of foreign residents from many different countries. The Japanese headquarters of many multinational companies are located in Kobe.

Kobe was founded sometime in the 8th century AD and can even boast that it served as the capital city of Japan, albeit for just a few months in 1180, after which the emperor returned to Kyoto. The modern city of Kobe was established in the late 19th century. It was heavily bombed during World War II, and the experience of that destruction led the residents of the city to campaign to have vessels carrying nuclear weapons banned from the harbor in 1975.

Left: Kobe is an important port city.

Right: Himeji Castle has been designated a UNESCO World Heritage Site.

Kobe's proximity to the Rokko mountain range, combined with its seaside setting, makes Kobe one of Japan's most scenic cities. Mount Rokko, at 3,070 feet (931 m), is the highest peak in the range. Kobe's seafront area features the landmark Port Tower, a steel structure in a modern geometric shape with sleek, curving lines. There are also two manmade islands in Kobe's harbor. They provide much-needed extra land area for the busy port's equipment and facilities.

One of Kobe's newest cultural events is called the Kobe Luminarie, the annual festival of lights, which has been held every year since the 1995 earthquake to celebrate the city's recovery and rebuilding following that disaster. In keeping with Kobe's cosmopolitanism and international connections, the first lights were donated by the government of Italy.

Himeji Castle, located in the city of Himeji near Kobe, is considered the finest surviving castle from Japanese feudal times. Himeji, with a population of half a million, is the second-largest city in Hyogo prefecture after Kobe. It is located less than an hour away from both Osaka and Kyoto on the super-fast *shinkansen* bullet train. Though the castle in its current state dates from 1609, there were earlier forts on this site from the 14th century. The fortress complex was gradually expanded by the feudal lords who occupied it.

Remarkably, the castle is still standing in its original condition, despite its location in an earthquake-prone region. It also managed to survive not one, but two bombs during World War II. The surrounding structures burned to the ground, but Himeji Castle itself, despite being constructed of wood, was spared. It boasts impressive and elaborate wooden interiors as well, and the surrounding gardens are particularly beautiful during the all-too-brief period each spring when the many cherry trees are in blossom.

The castle's tall stone foundations give it an important strategic advantage against invaders. Another defensive feature is the complex maze of pathways leading to the castle keep, intended to hamper the progress of invaders and thus make it easier for the castle's occupants to shoot at them.

Himeji Castle's brilliant white exterior is familiar all across Japan, thanks to the castle's frequent appearances in the media. Japanese people recognize Himeji Castle from many historical dramas on television. Many Western viewers, too, will have seen the castle in such productions as *Shogun*, starring Richard Chamberlain, and the James Bond adventure *You Only Live Twice*.

In addition to its status as the first official Japanese National Cultural Treasure, Himeji Castle is also a UNESCO World Heritage Site. It is the most visited castle in all of Japan, popular with Japanese as well as foreign tourists.

Left: A symbolic temple gate in Kobe.

Below: Rokko Island, a man-made island near Kobe, is home to busy wharves.

Hiroshima and Nagasaki

The cities of Hiroshima and Nagasaki are destined to be forever associated with the horrors of war. They are the only cities to have had atomic bombs used against them. However, despite their close links with one another in popular consciousness as a result of the events of World War II, they are not located particularly close to each other. In fact, the two cities are not even on the same island: Hiroshima is on Japan's largest island of Honshu, while Nagasaki is on the smaller, more southerly island of Kyushu.

Hiroshima is the largest city in the westernmost region of Japan's main Honshu island. Today, its population is over 1.1 million. Hiroshima is quite flat and is nearly at sea level. There is a good deal of industry in and around Hiroshima.

Hiroshima saw over 140,000 of its civilian residents killed by an atomic bomb that was dropped by the United States on August 6, 1945. This represented about half the population of the city. For the sake of comparison, conventional bombing resulted in about a 17 percent death rate in the same war.

Right: Memorial at Hiroshima Peace Park.

Below: A stark reminder of the horror of war at Hiroshima.

Hiroshima's Peace Memorial Park, including the Memorial Cenotaph, a massive stone arch, is a place for visitors from all over the world to reflect on the history of the city and the horrors of war. It is located in the area around the epicenter of the atomic explosion and includes the Peace Memorial Museum which is dedicated to the memory of those who lost their lives in World War II, as well as many other monuments. The museum graphically displays the horrible effects of the atomic bomb on the city and its inhabitants. Exhibits document Hiroshima's militaristic past and the process that led up to the dropping of the bomb. Audio guides are available in English and over a dozen other languages.

Hiroshima's former Industrial Promotion Hall is now known as the Atomic Bomb Dome. It is one of the few buildings around the epicenter of the explosion that partially survived the blast. Today it is the city's only remaining bomb-damaged building. It has been designated a UNESCO World Heritage Site.

Some other places of interest in modern-day Hiroshima include Hiroshima Castle, which was originally built in 1589 by the Mori clan. It was completely destroyed by the atomic bomb in 1945. In 1958 the concrete reconstruction of the castle was completed. It now houses a museum.

Shukkeien is a lovely traditional Japanese garden in Hiroshima which was originally constructed for the enjoyment of the local feudal lord in the 17th century. Shukkeien literally means "shrink scenery garden," as it displays a miniaturized version of a Chinese landscape with a pond, small islands, and bridges. Shukkeien is designed to be enjoyed by strolling around it in a circular route.

Right: Mountains form a picturesque backdrop to a town near Hiroshima.

Left: Despite the wartime devastation of Hiroshima, nature endures there.

The Nagasaki Peace Park commemorates the city's destruction by the atomic bomb that was dropped on the city on August 9, 1945. There are many statues in the park, including the massive Peace Statue.

Left: Folded paper cranes are an important symbol of peace.

Right: Painting with care and attention to detail in a Hiroshima park.

An interesting tourist attraction near Hiroshima is the small island of Miyajima. It can be reached by a short ferry ride from the city. Miyajima literally means "shrine island," and it is the site of the famous Itsukushima Shrine, which gives the island its name. Miyajima is considered by some to be a sacred island. Parts of the shrine stand on legs over the water, and the complex also features a famous "floating" *torii* gate, which was first constructed in the 6th century AD.

Visitors who time their visit with a high tide can experience the sight of the shrine and *torii* appearing to "float" over the water. It is also possible to spend the night on the island in order to enjoy the sight of the illuminated shrine. The shrine itself is closed at night, but the view is unforgettable. In fact, the scene is popularly ranked as one of Japan's three most beautiful views. Miyajima is also a popular honeymoon destination for newlywed Japanese couples. Populations of deer and monkeys roam around the island.

Nagasaki, located on the smaller island of Kyushu, is less than half the size of Hiroshima. Its present-day population is around 450,000. Nagasaki was founded prior to 1500, and its location by an excellent harbor made it a good trading and commercial center. Early in its history, Nagasaki had substantial contact with Portuguese traders. Some Portuguese products that were imported through Nagasaki, such as tobacco and some food items, became popular in Japan. After the Meiji Restoration in 1868, shipbuilding became an important industry in Nagasaki.

The Nagasaki Peace Park commemorates the city's destruction by the atomic bomb that was dropped on the city on August 9, 1945. There are many statues in the park, including the massive Peace Statue.

In the nearby Hypocenter Park, a monument with a black pillar marks the epicenter of the atomic explosion. The monument includes a list of the names of the bomb victims. The sobering Nagasaki A-Bomb Museum stands above the park.

Shikoku

The island of Shikoku, whose name literally means "four countries," is the smallest of Japan's four main islands. It is possible to travel by train from Honshu to Shikoku. Trains pass over the Inland Sea via the Seto-Ohashi Bridge, which was completed in 1986. There are other bridges for cars and trucks to use, or travelers can choose to go by ferry—or, of course, by air.

The largest city on Shikoku is Matsuyama. Matsuyama Castle is considered one of the most beautiful of Japan's few remaining original castles. It is situated on a steep, flat-topped hill. Matsuyama Castle is ununsual in that it is one of only three Japanese castles with multiple wings. Matsuyama Castle was constructed between 1602 and 1628. The current three-story castle tower was built in 1820 after the original five-story one was destroyed by a lightning strike.

Dogo Hot Spring, or *onsen*, is one of Japan's oldest and most famous natural hot springs. It is located on the outskirts of Matsuyama. The main attraction is a wooden public bathhouse, which dates from 1894 during the Meiji era. The elegant complex offers tea, Japanese sweets, and private rooms where guests can relax after their bath.

Left: Shikoku is one of Japan's smaller main islands so the sea is always nearby.

Right: A view over Hiwachi on Shikoku Island.

Shikoku is also famous for its 88-temple pilgrimage route. Most modern-day pilgrims choose to travel by bus, instead of the old-fashioned method of going on foot. The tradition began with the story of the Buddhist monk Kukai, who was born on Shikoku in 774 AD. According to legend, it is said that Kukai visited all 88-temples that form the pilgrimage route. However, Kukai actually mentions visiting only two of them in his own writings. In addition to the 88 "official" temples of the pilgrimage, there are over 200 other, smaller temples on Shikoku that are not considered part of the official 88. In order to complete the pilgrimage, it is not necessary to visit the temples in order—in fact, in some cases it is even considered lucky to travel in reverse order. The walking route is approximately 750 miles (1,200 km) long, and it can take anywhere from 30 to 60 days to complete.

Left: A bridge over a river in Shikoku.

Far left: Buddhist mantras inscribed on a temple wall in Shikoku.

Fukuoka

Fukuoka is the capital and largest city of the island of Kyushu, the southernmost of Japan's four main islands. Fukuoka is one of Japan's ten most populated cities. Because of its proximity to the Asian mainland—it is closer to Seoul than to Tokyo—Fukuoka has long been an important harbor city and trading center, as well as a point of contact for foreigners, both friendly and otherwise. For instance, invading Mongol forces chose Fukuoka as their landing point in the 12th century.

Fukuoka is home to Shofukuji, considered to be the oldest Zen temple in all of Japan. It was originally constructed in 1195 by a priest named Eisai shortly after he had returned from China. It was Eisai's aim to introduce the Rinzai Zen sect to Japan. However, the beautiful wooden buildings visitors see today are not original, because the structures were destroyed by fire several times over the centuries.

Left: The city of Fukuoka is actually closer to Seoul, South Korea, than to Tokyo.

Right: Cherry blossoms in bloom in Fukuoka.

Northern Honshu

The northern part of Japan's main island of Honshu is relatively sparsely populated, at least in comparison to the south. There are not so many huge metropolitan areas here.

Miyagi Prefecture, on the Pacific coast in northern Honshu, has Sendai as its largest city. Not far from Sendai is the famous location of Matsushima, which is referred to as one of the three most scenic views of Japan. Matsushima possesses a bay filled with 260 small islands covered in pine groves.

There is a well-known haiku poem about Matsushima that clearly conveys the breathtaking beauty and serenity of the Matsushima view. The poet's name has been lost through the passage of time, but his original Japanese version can by enjoyed just as well by English speakers:

Matsushima, ah!
A-ah, Matsushima, ah!
Matsushima, ah!

Nikko is a small city located in the mountains north of Tokyo. Nikko is a popular destination for Japanese and international tourists, who travel there to view the mausoleum of *shogun* Tokugawa Ieyasu. He was the founder of the Tokugawa shogunate, which ruled in Japan from 1600 until the Meiji Restoration in 1868. There are also many famous hot springs, called *onsen* in Japanese, in the area. The mountains west of the city are part of Nikko National Park. This park contains some of Japan's most spectacular waterfalls and scenic trails.

Left: Matsushima is one of the best-loved views in Japan.

Far left: Nikko is a popular destination for tourists from Japan and abroad.

Nagano and Matsumoto

The city of Nagano is the capital of Nagano Prefecture in western Honshu. Nagano is most famous for the Zenko-ji Buddhist temple, which overlooks the city. The Zenko-ji temple was established some 1,400 years ago. It houses what many people believe to be the first Buddhist statue ever brought to Japan. A copy of the statue is displayed in public every seven years for a few days. The next opportunity to view the statue will be in 2010. Most recently rebuilt in 1707, Zenko-ji's main hall has a tunnel in its basement. This tunnel is completely dark. Visitors go into the tunnel and try to find and touch the "key to paradise," which is attached to the wall. The key is said to grant enlightenment to anyone who touches it in the total darkness.

Nagano was the host city for the 1998 Winter Olympics and Paraolympics. Many of the former facilities can still be viewed in and around the city. The Olympic facilities include the White Ring, which was the venue for some of the skating events. It now serves as a gymnasium. The Big Hat was one of the two ice hockey venues and is now a multipurpose hall, while the Aqua Wing was the second venue for ice hockey and has now been converted into an indoor swimming pool. Perhaps the best place to experience Nagano's Olympic past, however, is M-Wave, the venue for the speed skating events. M-Wave is now a multi-purpose arena and also houses the Nagano Olympic Museum, where visitors can see items such as the Olympic torch and an official Japanese Olympic team uniform.

Right: Mountains near Nagano, the site of the 1998 Winter Olympics.

Below: The natural hot water springs near Nagano get all kinds of visitors!

Matsumoto is the second-largest city in Nagano Prefecture. Its most famous feature is Matsumoto Castle, one of Japan's most beautiful original castles. Matsumoto Castle's main tower and smaller second turret were built between 1592 and 1614. Because there were still many battles being fought around that time, both were well defended. In 1635, when military threats had subsided, a third turret for moon viewing was added to the castle. It was virtually without defensive structural elements.

Matsumoto is also an ideal starting point for trips into the mountainous region commonly known as the Japanese Alps.

Northern Nagano Prefecture has more than half a dozen hot springs. The area is most famous for its so-called "snow monkeys," or Japanese macaques. These monkeys are indigenous to Japan, and many live in Jigokudani Monkey Park. There is a hot spring pool in the park that is reserved for exclusive use by the monkeys. They love to lounge around in the naturally warm water, especially in the cold winter months, when the air temperature drops below freezing and the valley is covered by a thick layer of snow. Hot springs for use by humans can be found farther down the valley.

Above: Chairlifts at a ski resort near Nagano, the Olympic city.

Left: Festive flags on a Nagano street.

Hokkaido

Hokkaido is the most northerly of Japan's four main islands. It is the second largest but also the least developed of the four main islands. Hokkaido is connected to the largest island of Honshu by the underwater Seikan Tunnel.

Hokkaido's winters can be quite harsh, with lots of snowfall, temperatures below freezing, and frozen seas. In summer, it does not get as hot and humid as the other parts of Japan. Hokkaido attracts many lovers of outdoor sports and activities, in summer as well as winter. Skiing, snowboarding, hiking, bicycling, and camping are all popular pursuits. There is also a popular hot spring resort

at Noboribetsu, which is located in the southern part of Hokkaido.

Some residents of Hokkaido are members of the Ainu, a distinct ethnic group indigenous to Hokkaido. The origins of the Ainu are unknown, but it is believed that they probably traveled to Hokkaido from the island of Sakhalin or the Kamchatka Peninsula, both of which are now part of Russia. The Ainu people have their own cultural traditions and religious practices. The Ainu language is completely different from Japanese. As a result of cultural assimilation, the number of speakers of Ainu is extremely low, and the language is in danger

Below: The Noboribetsu samurai village gives visitors a view of Japan's feudal past.

Above: A place for quiet contemplation in Hokkaido.

of dying out. There is, however, a movement to revitalize its use.

Sapporo is the capital city of Hokkaido and Japan's fifth-largest city. Sapporo is also one of the nation's newest major cities. The name Sapporo means "important river flowing through a plain" in the Ainu language. Sapporo has grown significantly since 1857, when the population numbered just seven people. Its growth was the result of administrative planning: at the start of the Meiji Period, Sapporo was chosen to be the island's administrative center. Development was planned according to the advice of foreign experts. As a result, Sapporo's street layout was based on a North American style rectangular street system.

Sapporo became world-famous in 1972 when the Winter Olympics were held there. Today, the city is also known for the brand of beer that is brewed there, as well as the annual snow festival held in February.

From the snowy north to the subtropical south, Japan contains an amazing variety of landscapes, climates, industries, and cultural events. The next chapter explains some of Japan's unique traditions and practices in more detail.

Cultural Heritage

Like its physical environment, Japan's culture is rich in contrast. Traces of its intriguing traditions still endure in today's fast-paced lifestyles.

Along with the geisha, the samurai is perhaps the most distinctive Japanese figure, possessing a consuming honor and commitment—a purity of vision—not attributed to the soldiers of other cultures. Despite the image commonly held today of a refined, noble warrior, the samurai had humble origins. The term originally referred to a servant, and until the 14th century few of them were literate. At the end of the first millennium, Japan was wracked by war, with most of the conflict over the island's scarce farmland. Fearful landowners needed men to defend their estates, and the samurai took on the task. But they soon grew in power and status, and rose above the ranks of hired muscle. The culmination of the Gempei War in 1185 saw the Minamoto defeat the Taira clan, and a few years later install its leader, Yoritomo, as shogun, a kind of military dictator, rendering the office of emperor a powerless symbol, which it was to remain for six and a half centuries. The samurai had reached the top of Japan's social system.

The samurai might be synonymous with his sword, but he was far more than a mere swordsman. From the 14th century Samurai were encouraged to become literate and cultured. Their code of honor, something like the European idea of chivalry, was bushido, which held up frugality, loyalty, mastery of martial arts, and honor to the death as its central tenets. And it is this last part that is the most shocking element of the samurai ethos: their willingness to make the ultimate sacrifice for failure. Bushido has it that if an adherent falls below expectations or is captured by the enemy, he can avoid disgrace with seppuku, also known as hara-kiri, or ritual suicide by disembowelment. It was an agonizing death. Often a comrade would try to limit the suffering by decapitating his dying ally immediately after it had begun. As well as absolving the deceased of any failure, there was also the practical consideration that *seppuku* was likely to be more bearable than any torture the enemy might inflict. The honorable suicide tradition survived in Japanese culture, with indebted businessmen and kamikaze pilots taking the same route in modern times.

Their noble lives and dramatic deaths have made the samurai ideal movie fare. Perhaps the most acclaimed example is the 1954 classic *The Seven Samurai* by Japanese director Akira Kurosawa, himself descended from a line of warriors, but samurai films and culture have influenced filmmakers as diverse as John Sturges, Sergio Leone, and Quentin Tarantino.

In the 1850s, Japan's cultural isolation was terminated by its first trade with the United States. The office of emperor soon had its full power restored. The first incumbent, Meiji, not only opened the army up to anyone, but also brought in a law that banned the wearing of swords, spelling the end of the samurai era. But while the real-life samurai might be consigned to history, the myth lives on, not only on the big screen and in literature and tradition, but also in the values of honor, self-discipline and self-sacrifice still held up in Japan today.

War and isolation have been the defining forces in shaping Japan's history. Its island status was instrumental in its destiny—although it did not start out as an island. Japan's first hunter-gatherer inhabitants are thought to have lived there over 100,000 years ago, when the country was still attached to mainland Asia. In time it separated and drifted away, and the technology improved, with the help of early innovation from Asia. Separate states sprang up, and then unified, creating a powerful political authority. From the last few centuries of the BC era, the country was ruled by an emperor.

Above: Culture and refinement became important elements to the samurai.

Left: Samurai life has been accurately depicted as brutal.

The Samurai's code of honor was *bushido*, which emphasized frugality, loyalty, mastery of martial arts, and honor to the death as its central tenets.

Japan progressed largely by adapting things from its huge neighbor: language, a government system, technology, and religion. The Japanese court was focusing on the arts, but at the expense of its authority, when the Minamoto family seized power in 1185, heralding the start of seven centuries of feudalism, with one military leader, or *shogun*, often deposing his predecessor. Meanwhile, there were other threats: the Mongols were trying to invade and the country was wracked by civil war.

Although Japan had benefited immeasurably from its dealings with foreign nations, in 1639, the shogun Tokugawa Ieyasu installed a policy prohibiting all but a few outsiders from visiting. The ban lasted for two and half centuries before succumbing to world pressure, particularly from United States Navy Commodore Matthew Perry, who persuaded the Japanese to start trading with certain nations. This spelled the end of the feudal era, and the office of emperor, which had been a mere figurehead for centuries, regained its full power. Making up for lost time, Japan set about effecting a rigorous process of modernization. It also expanded its territory through military victories. Despite playing a minor role for the Allies in World War I, in the next world war it joined Germany and Italy, carrying out the famous attack on Pearl Harbor. Fierce resistance led to the United States dropping two atomic bombs on Hiroshima and Nagasaki and Japan's unconditional surrender.

Following some liberalization under American occupation, Japan began to rebuild itself and trade with other nations. It has emerged from the ashes of defeat in World War II as one of the most technologically advanced countries in the world and the second richest after the United States.

Left: Japanese texts are part of a rich literary tradition.

Right: The unique Japanese sense of style.

Left: Geisha are a much-misunderstood phenomenon to outsiders.

Right: Today, only a thousand or two geisha are believed to remain.

The Geisha's striking make-up was created using a layer of wax with white powder for the face, charcoal eye makeup, and crystallized sugar for the lips.

Indeed, costume was one way that geisha could be distinguished from prostitutes, as the latter could not afford to spend so much time getting dressed and undressed. The kimono bow, or *obi*, provided a clue: prostitutes tied theirs at the front, geisha at the back. Few geisha had children and few got married—if they did they had to quit. In place of a husband, the women would have a wealthy patron, or *danna*, often married, who supported the considerable financial costs of the geisha. It is said that the danna would sometimes purchase her *mizuage*, or virginity, which could be auctioned at a young age—although many deny this was widespread and the practice has now been outlawed.

It remains just one of the many mysteries of the geisha. Like magicians, with whom they shared a code of silence, everything was about illusion. A geisha could be angry, hateful, distraught inside but must remain ever the composed and charming helper. The illusion must never be broken.

Japanese clothing

Japanese clothing varies to reflect the season, event, level of formality required, age and marital status (in the case of women) of the wearer. The standard garment is the kimono, which in fact translates to "something worn" or "clothes." However, the word eventually came to refer solely to the long gown with wide, full-length sleeves, secured with a sash, or *obi*. The kimono is descended from a style of Chinese dress known as *hanfu*, which the Japanese characteristically refashioned in their own style, following the severing of relations with China. They applied typical Japanese dedication to the garment— women of the court would wear up to 20 kimono at once for ceremonies. Once the samurai adopted the style of dress, it soon spread down from the nobility to the rest of society.

Since the end of the 12th century, the robe has changed very little. The manufacturing techniques of traditional kimono have stayed the same, although modern technology now allows mass production too. Kimono are typically one size and handmade; their fabric too is made by hand. At one time they would have been taken apart entirely to be washed, and then re-stitched, although this is no longer common. However, a quality kimono requires a lot of work, and this is reflected in the price: it is not unusual for a good kimono today to cost more than $10,000, perhaps double that with all the necessary accessories included. The labor and cash involved means that kimono are never wasted. Instead, old garments are remade into smaller kimono, the material used for "spare parts" to fix up others or to make bags or covers, or put to various other uses dreamed up by enterprising and economical Japanese. Some now choose to make their own kimono, although this is a laborious and difficult process. One group denied access to standard kimono is Japan's sumo wrestlers. The garment is part of their dress code when appearing in public, but with normal models made from a single piece of fabric, the sumo's hefty size presents a problem, and they must commission their kimono specially.

Left: The Japanese ideal of conformity is evident in its people's attire for special festivals.

Right: Zori, brought back to America by returning servicemen, are said to have been the inspiration for flip-flops.

Bottom: Color coordination is an important motif in Japanese fashion.

A quality kimono for formal wear is made of hand-dyed silk, with cotton and polyester garments worn on casual occasions. Color, accessories, and *kamon*, or family symbols, may all increase the level of formality inherent in a garment. A young unmarried woman's kimono typically has large sleeves at the wrist, sometimes a foot and a half wide. Older women and men tend to wear simpler, more somber garments. As in most areas of traditional Japanese life, Western styles have permeated the isolation, and kimono are now seldom spotted among the jeans, t-shirts, and sneakers favored by Japanese youth. Kimono now tend to be reserved for special occasions, such as weddings, funerals, New Year festivities and tea ceremonies, as well as some martial arts that have retained high levels of ritual and tradition. When worn, they are tied—in one of more than 300 different ways—by an *obi*, with undergarments such as a shirt or slip, a lightweight jacket on top, a coordinating purse, and elaborate hairstyle.

Footwear, too, must be appropriate, even if sometimes it is barely visible under the kimono itself. *Zori*, which should be coordinated with the rest of the outfit, are wooden or vinyl sandals, worn with special socks called *tabi*, designed with a split to accommodate the strap that goes between the toes. American soldiers returning from World War II brought *zori* with them as souvenirs, and this is thought to have inspired the design of rubber flip-flops.

The other essential Japanese accessory is the fan, a symbolic object whose top connotes the start of life and ribs the various paths to prosperity. It features in ceremonies, traditional dancing, and is also commonly given as a gift. Actors often used fans as props, nobles carried them as status symbols, and even generals took them onto the battlefield, both as a form of insignia and also to use as a pointer. In contrast to much of Japanese culture, which was entirely imported from China, fans also went the other way—many folding fan designs originated in ancient Japan and reached Europe via the Asian continent. The typical constituent parts—bamboo, paper, and silk—are also indigenous.

Right: The ribs of the fan symbolize the various paths to prosperity.

Below: Fans served as props on the stage, status symbols, and even battlefield insignia.

As in most areas of traditional Japanese life, Western styles have permeated and kimono are now seldom spotted among the jeans, t-shirts, and sneakers favored by Japanese youth.

Family life

Children are precious in Japan. That statement might sound facile—after all, children are precious in every culture. But the demographic specifics mean that a Japanese child is truly special. The country has one of the lowest birth rates in the world, and that, combined with the longevity of its population, means that the balance is slowly but significantly tipping in favor of the old. When a phenomenon becomes too serious to ignore, the Japanese give it a name. The country now fears that it is heading towards *shoshika*, a society without children. It was projected that unless the situation could be halted, by the middle of the 21st century, Japan's population would be reduced by 20 percent, and half of it would be elderly. 2006 saw the first rise in the birth rate in six years, giving cause for optimism, but the child retains its venerated position in Japanese society. Sons and daughters are celebrated in annual festivals.

While government policies and unwelcome traditional expectations of women have contributed toward the low fertility rate, another reason is the Japanese emphasis on education. A mother can devote time to one or two children, nurturing them to a level of learning she could not manage with a bigger brood. In a regimented system, good grades led to a place in a reputable university and onto a job for life at a top company. Few parents would risk jeopardizing that by overextending. The Japanese school system instills a strong work ethic in its charges, encouraging respect, the importance of the group, and diligence as the path to success. Cramming and pressure have been the norm. But falling numbers of potential students are changing the nature of the system, and it remains to be seen how Japan will respond.

Above: With Japan's low birth rate, young children are a precious commodity.

Right: Though no longer everyday wear, traditional Japanese dress often makes an appearance at festivals.

Below: Education is emphasized by parents desperate for their children to get the best start in life.

The smallness of families has had an effect on the habits of children as they grow older. Masahiro Yamaguchi of Tokyo Metropolitan University labeled them "parasite singles," twenty-somethings who stay living at home long after the end of their education, receiving an allowance from their generous mom and dad. The parents, in turn, are happy to house their adult offspring in return for the sense of security they feel, knowing there is someone there to look after them if they become ill. A few of the parasite singles may become *hikikomori*, recluses who shut themselves off from the world. But for the majority, living under the parents' roof is a healthy and comfortable choice.

Perhaps another benefit in having an older son or daughter around the house is having someone to help you get to grips with the latest gadget. Young Japanese are hugely technology-savvy. Many use their latest generation cellphones to go online for hours every day—to the extent that sitting at a computer, or using a cellphone to make a call is now considered old-fashioned. But the youth of Japan has always been ripe territory for a craze, whether it was Tamagotchi, the cyberpet that cried and died, Pokémon, Hello Kitty, loose socks or "Gothic Lolita" fashion. Sometimes the excitement and suggestibility that leads to the eccentric concepts that race around the world wanders into dark territory—a spate of deaths of young people who had formed suicide clubs over the internet shocked the world and posed hard questions about the Japanese psyche.

But most of it is fun: a defining aesthetic of young Japanese style is *kawaii*, or cuteness. Cosmetics and designer goods now find an eager market there. So too Western celebrities—David Beckham and Michael Jackson were met with rapturous welcomes on recent visits to the country. Perhaps some of this is a reaction to the rigidity of traditional Japanese values. Is this evident in a new generation of *furita*, part-time or temporary workers, who have eschewed the time-consuming work ethic of their parents to bum around between casual jobs? As Western values increasingly break through into Japan's traditionally isolated society, its young people stand at a crossroads.

Japanese festivals

Offering respite from the strict Japanese working culture, festivals are often frenetic and raucous affairs. They are also numerous. Because the vast majority of shrines celebrate their own local festival, or *matsuri*, there will almost always be some kind of celebration going on somewhere, many of which last for days. Such events often include a procession, which sees the shrine's deity make its annual departure from its habitat to be paraded through the town, along with elaborate floats. Despite the typically religious nature of the *matsuri*, the atmosphere is more like a carnival, with souvenirs and food sold from street stalls and live music, karaoke and sumo wrestling to entertain the crowds. These events so capture the public interest that the most popular often appear on television. Seasonal changes, life milestones, the natural world, religion, and honoring historical figures, ancestors, and family members all provide a reason for the Japanese to get together and make merry. And while there are some festivals at which quiet contemplation is called for, the majority are usually held in a party spirit, with food, drink, music, and revelry all part of the deal.

Left: Japanese celebrations often include a historical element.

Right: Lanterns are typical décor for celebrations.

Over: The frequency and duration of matsuri *means that there is almost always a festival going on somewhere.*

The biggest festival is held for New Year, or *oshougatsu*. In a departure from the custom in its neighboring nations, Japan's citizens no longer mark Chinese New Year, but party along with the West on January 1. In the lead-up, business people try to pay off their debts, and it is common to give small gifts to people who have helped you during the year, such as a teacher. In recognition of the hard work put in all year by staff, companies throw *bonenkai*, or "forget the year" parties. Forgetting the night is certainly a possibility, as food and drink are often consumed in copious amounts. Invitations are extended not only to employees, but also company associates, so a Japanese worker whose job involves liaising

Below: Festive lanterns decorate a backdrop of cherry blossoms.

with other firms can end up having a rather tiring party season. Housewives, meanwhile, are equally busy, preparing the food that will be enjoyed by friends and family until January 3, during which time schools and offices remain closed. Many of the dishes eaten then are specific to the time of year, and several have symbolic meanings, such as black beans, said to bring good luck and success, and fish roe, a harbinger of fertility. Women and children can often be seen in traditional kimono around this holiday period. At the exact moment the New Year begins, temple bells ring out 108 times, to combat the 108 sins in Buddhism.

Children feature prominently in many festivals. For *hina matsuri*, held on March 3, a family prays for its daughter's wellbeing, and that she may find a good husband. Exquisitely dressed miniature dolls signifying members of the nobility are arranged on a tiered shelf. The day afterwards they must be taken down and put away—to fail to do so means the daughter's wedding will be delayed, according to Japanese superstition. The sons' equivalent was on May 5, although today children of both genders are involved with *kodomo-no-hi*. This time the doll was in the form of a warrior, symbolizing the parents' hope that their son would be brave and successful. Kites in the shape of a carp, the symbol of strength for its defiant swimming against the river, are also hung up as decoration.

At the other end of the scale is *keiro-no-hi*, respect for the elderly day. Held, appropriately, in fall, the festival sees the Tokyo authorities honor any citizen who has reached the age of 100 with a gift, while children also make presents for their grandparents. Japan's impressively high life expectancy means that there are plenty of recipients.

Right: Cherry blossoms are reflected in the glassy water surface.

Sports and martial arts

Violent pursuits have often been viewed in the West as the preserve of the common class. Boxing, for example, was the working man's sport in Western countries, a means for a youth to fight his way out of the poverty and deprivation of his childhood. By contrast, the Japanese tradition of martial arts has always been held in high esteem, as the occupation of noblemen. The country's warrior caste was the highest level of society, and the lower orders were not permitted to bear weapons. Samurai had to excel in both armed and unarmed combat, and when members of the profession turned en masse to Buddhism, the pursuit of distinction on the battlefield became a way to achieve spiritual goals. Respect for the dignified fighter persists today, chiming as it does with Japanese ideals of self-discipline, dedication, and mastery.

The high standing of martial arts was also due in part to the island nation's isolation. While military technology typically advances rapidly, in secluded Japan the development of weapons unfolded at a slower pace, and simpler weapons and unarmed combat could be studied and mastered over a longer period. The end of the samurai era coincided with the rise of modern weapon technology, and Japan's martial arts began to decline. But the end of the 19th century brought about a revival, thanks to *Dai Nippon Budo Kai*, or the Great Japan Martial Arts Association, which managed to get the sports onto the school curriculum and thus guarantee further generations of participants. The resurgence was briefly interrupted after the end of World War II, when the occupying American forces banned martial arts, fearing that they were too closely linked with Japanese nationalism. The ban lasted five years, after which they were once again permitted, this time with the emphasis on their sporting rather than military characteristics.

The Japanese tradition of martial arts has always been held in high esteem, as the occupation of noblemen. Traditionally the warrior caste was the highest level of society.

Opposite: Martial arts are taught as a way to impart discipline.

Below: The sword was elevated by its association with the samurai.

The master-apprentice relationship has always been central to the passing down of the Japanese martial arts tradition, where the wise elder painstakingly grooms the respectful youngster, teaching him as much about life and values as about combat techniques. Perhaps the first representation of that bond for many young adults was the 1984 film *The Karate Kid*. In the movie, the hero's mentor, Mr. Miyagi, is a blend of wisdom and wit, a gentle demeanor disguising great strength—the Japanese ideal. Kung-fu movies are a genre in their own right, and martial artists like Bruce Lee broke out of the niche to become mainstream Hollywood stars.

Karate, which means "empty hand," is a combination of martial arts from the Japanese island of Okinawa and China. It was popularized by Gichin Funakoshi, who gave demonstrations of the art at government-sponsored exhibitions in 1917 and 1922, after which it began to be taught in schools. The *kyuu* ranking system and the white karate suits became features around this time. Essentially, the sport consists of delivering sharp punches and kicks from a fixed posture to the opponent's pressure-sensitive points, although modern karate also sees no-contact and light-contact competitions held. The most iconic move is the karate chop, a sharp downward blow with the side of the hand, which can, when delivered by an expert, smash boards and even bricks. A physicist from the Massachusetts Institute of Technology describes it as "one of the most efficient human movements ever conceived." Over 23 million people worldwide are thought to practice karate.

Right: Karate has millions of participants worldwide.

Judo is one of the most internationally popular of the Japanese martial arts, with five million practitioners around the world. The word itself means "the gentle way," and the sport shares the spiritual aspects of many other martial arts. It came about at the end of the 19th century, the brainchild of Jigoro Kano, the son of a family of sake brewers, who brought together elements of other sports to make a form of wrestling that was more freestyle than some other martial arts. Judo's beginnings are depicted in the 1943 film *Sanshiro Sugata*, which features the master-protégé relationship and stand-off tournament in much the same way that *The Karate Kid* would, four decades later.

Judo is often described as a descendant of jujitsu. The art of compliance, which the term means, developed as a way to defeat a more heavily-armed adversary, and predominantly involves indirect, counterattacking moves such as joint locks, restraint, blocks, and throws, rather than direct hits, the aim being to turn an opponent's force back on him. Some small weapons also feature. Another jujitsu offshoot, which employs similar methods, is the self-defense system of aikido. Timing and positioning are vital in outmaneuvering the opponent, and the aikido participant has been described as moving like an empty-handed swordsman. Here, the aim is to restrain an opponent, rather than severely harm him or her. The term aikido means "the way of spiritual harmony," and self-control and mental calmness are the basis of the sport. Respect and courtesy also form a significant part of the training. While the skills involved in aikido were in use as early as the 14th century, the sport took on its current aspect in the early 1900s.

Above: Sumo has retained many of its traditions, with the referee dressing as a Shinto priest.

Sumo wrestlers typically live in strict camps, and follow their huge food consumption by immediately going to bed to boost their weight gain.

Right: Sumo wrestlers retain their portliness by following large meals with a nap.

The unofficial national sport, sumo, has origins dating back as far as the BC era, according to Japan's first written records. Participants were generally hefty, the aim being to collapse your opponent or force him out of the circle. Sumo wrestlers typically live in strict camps, and follow their huge food consumption by immediately going to bed to boost their weight gain. The sport's initial purpose was entertainment for the Shinto gods. Emperor Shomu was a fan, and from the 8th century he hosted official matches. It was picked up by both the religious and military branches of Japanese life. Soldiers did sumo as part of their training, while Shinto festivals also featured sumo contests. The religious connection is still evident today in the uniform of the referee, which resembles that of a Shinto priest. The clapping, stamping, and salt-throwing that precede the match have also endured for centuries.

Sumo may be regarded as the national sport, but for many, swordsmanship is the king of martial arts. Elevated by the samurai, the *katana*, or Japanese long sword, is the stuff of legend. In times of peace, the Japanese concentrated on making their swords artistic; in times of war, practical concerns such as durability and ease of production came to the fore. The first swords, which were in use in the 3rd and 4th centuries, had straight blades. Curved swords came into being in Japan about three centuries later, some say as a result of technological know-how imported from China. The samurai's adoption of Buddhist thinking led to the transformation of the sword from a mere weapon to an object encompassing the ideas of spirituality and growth. A descendant of swordsmanship, *kendo*, a kind of fencing, translates to "the way of the sword." Bamboo weapons and lightweight armor, which were introduced in the 18th century, made the sport quicker and safer. Its links to the samurai mean that *kendo* retains a great deal of ritual.

Many of the martial arts are brought together in the figure of the ninja, an assassin or spy trained in the art of stealth. The ninja's origins are in the feudal Japan of the 14th century, when he would likely have been employed by the shogun to carry out nefarious missions such as sabotage or execution—all of the dirty work that a respectable ruler could not delegate to his ordinary men. The ninja were the other side of the samurai coin: though both were highly efficient fighting machines, one was noble, loyal and self-sacrificing, the other furtive and rebellious. Ninja ranks also included women, who could enter powerful households in the guise of servants for spying assignments. Their weapons were everyday tools that could be disguised, but they also employed high-profile diversion tactics like smoke bombs and firecrackers, as well as sophisticated ruses to throw pursuers off their scent, such as wooden shoe pads with indentations that resembled animal paw prints. The ninja's chief asset—secrecy—is also the one thing that keeps us from fully understanding this uniquely Japanese phenomenon even today.

Many of the martial arts are brought together in the figure of the ninja, an assassin or spy trained in the art of stealth. The ninja's chief asset— secrecy—means the history of ninja is still shrouded in mystery.

Left: Stealthy and cunning, the ninja is the other side of the samurai coin.

Above: Alternating periods of war and peace contributed to the artistry and durability of the Japanese sword.

Theater and cultural pursuits

Like many aspects of Japanese culture, the theater had two main branches, one for the aristocracy and one for the commoners. The ruling class saw drama as a way to instruct the lower orders in the traits of loyalty and self-sacrifice—although the outcome was not always as they desired. Popular theater is said to have begun in the early 17th century, when the priest Okuni quit her Shinto temple to open a playhouse in Kyoto. The exaggerated performances, gory plots, and witty puns delighted audiences. As well as plays featuring real actors, puppet shows were also staged, and both advanced in quality to such an extent that nobles also deigned to attend. Whether they found that the theater had had the edifying effect on the commoners that they had hoped is not so certain. Fights were not uncommon, and some time around 1683 a law was passed banning swords in the theater. The samurai refused to attend swordless, and, after the theaters had been robbed of their high-class audiences, the standard of the shows dropped so much that Genshiro, an early 19th century Japanese playwright and critic, later wrote that "the theater in Japan had reached the lowest depth of vulgarity," a nadir which lasted for nearly 200 years.

The theater for the upper class has a longer history. *Noh* plays, which are musical dramas, reached their peak in the 14th century. Male actors wore elaborate costumes and masks in day-long theatrical displays—although several different plays of about an hour each would be staged. *Noh* plays were mostly tragedies, and touched on highbrow themes like Buddhism. Light relief in between came in the form of short farces called *kiogen*. The actors, singers, and musicians never rehearsed together. Each one would practice his own part either alone, or with a senior mentor from the troupe—in much the same way as a martial artist would learn from a master. The logic behind this was the *ichi-go ichi-e* principle, which translates as "one time, one meeting," in line with the Buddhist idea of transcendence.

Above: A noh mask breaks down a character to its essential elements.

Right: The elderly are one of the five main categories of noh mask representations.

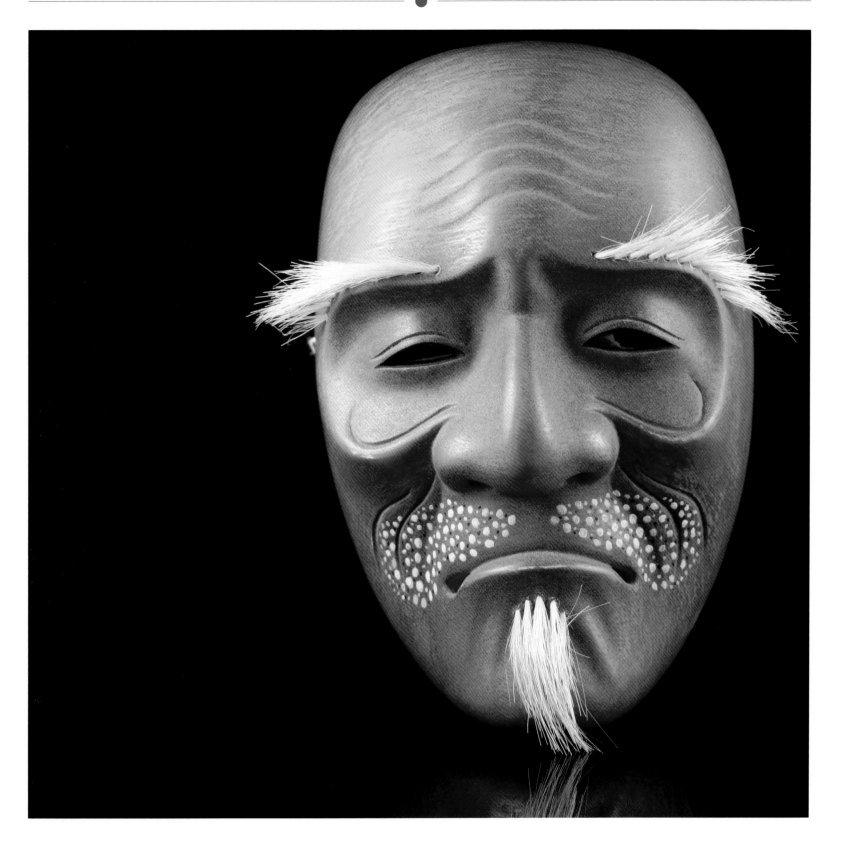

More important than a prop, more important than a costume, was the mask in Japanese *noh* theater. Its status was reflected by the fact that only the main character wore one. The mask had a key role in believability. Today women are finally making inroads into *noh*, but traditionally it was a male-dominated pastime, and a male actor would often play a female role. A mask would add to his credibility in the part. Masks also appealed to the Japanese love of simplicity and symbolism. They would convey a stylized image of the character, breaking it down to its essential elements. This was intended to be a truer representation than an actor could muster. Naturally through the course of the play the character would go on a tumultuous emotional journey and be required to communicate conflicting emotions. As a result, the face of the mask would be crafted in a neutral expression, leaving it to the actor's individual talent to invest this blank canvas with feeling. He did, however, have some tricks to help him. Some *noh* masks, especially among those created for female characters, were designed so that a small modification in the position of the wearer's head could alter the lighting or angle in such a way as to convey different emotions. This sat well with Buddhist concepts of frugality in movement and expression.

Author and curator Gregory Irvine describes the process by which the actor gets into the part and bonds with his mask as an early form of method acting: "After donning his sumptuous costume the actor seats himself before a mirror and studies the mask, becoming one with the character he is about to perform. The mask is then tied onto his head, any wig or necessary headgear is put on and he stands before a full-length mirror, letting the mask take over his own personality before he is led to the stage." This fits with the Japanese ethic of group accomplishment over individual glory: the actor would have sought to disappear into an effective rendition of his role, rather than seek to claim individual kudos for his performance.

Left: Vibrant and elaborate costumes are an essential part of Japanese theater.

Above: Actors rehearse separately to ensure that each performance is unique.

Noh masks can be broken down into five main representations: gods, demons, men, women, and the elderly. Early examples were used in religious rituals—at one point mask production was undertaken by Buddhist priests as a hobby—but they soon spread through secular theater and society. The very first Japanese masks were used in the Jomon period, from 10,000 to 300 BC, and were made of clay or cloth. Wood later proved much more efficient, and over the past few centuries the production process has changed little. A crucial element was weight: the main actor would have to wear his mask for over an hour at a time, so it needed to be small and light. The mask would be fashioned from a piece of cypress wood, or *hinoki*. Holes were bored to allow the wearer to see and breathe, after which the item would be coated in gesso and glue, then sanded and finally painted, with the hair and borders of the eyes done in black.

Perhaps the high cultural value placed on the mask has informed some of the conduct of modern Japan. Many American visitors have noticed Japanese people's reluctance to make eye contact. For a woman to give a broad smile in Japan is considered an indiscretion, and many will cover their faces when struck by something amusing. These and other behaviors have contributed to the stereotype of the "inscrutable" Japanese. In this respect, the mask remains in use.

Above left: Japanese instruments show typical delicacy and style.

Below left: Like other performing arts, music filtered down from the elite to the masses.

Far left: Traditional Japanese music now shares the scene with J-pop and Western hits.

Hobbies and Leisure

With a famously demanding work schedule and high-pressure education system, Japanese hobbies and leisure-time pursuits play a vital part in giving their practitioners some downtime, a release from the frenetic pace of everyday life. Devotees typically go about their hobbies and leisure pursuits with the same degree of commitment that they bring to other aspects of their lives, and the effects of this are evident in the high art forms that have resulted, many of which have caught on around the world.

Music in Japan has been shaped by various cultures: the Chinese, the imperial court, the samurai, Buddhism and *noh* theater. Early popular Japanese songs were political or social in theme, and much music of the time was categorized by the region from which it had come. An important distinction is that the country did not see music as something to be enjoyed in isolation. Instead it was a constituent part of a bigger idea: court ritual, theater, dance, or acrobatics. Religion was another context for music. Buddhist chanting was intended to bring about serenity and self-transcendence, and was not in any way about performance. Two periods proved most fallow in the development of Japanese music. The long stretch of uninterrupted peace of the Heian period from the 8th to the 12th century allowed the Japanese the leisure to develop their own style, distinctive from the Asian music they had co-opted. And the 16th century saw a democratization of the performing arts, which had filtered down from exclusively court pursuits to something for all to enjoy. Today, many of the traditional musical forms survive, alongside J-pop, Japan's version of Western pop. Sony and Yamaha are two of the biggest names in modern music, while karaoke has been arguably the biggest democratizing force for amateur vocals.

Above: Manga betrays obvious Disney influences.

Right: The logic puzzle that took the world by storm: Sudoku.

Far right: Leisure and culture represent an escape from the demanding bustle of everyday life.

Harmony between humankind and nature is the basis of one of the Japanese's great passions: gardens. The perfect balance of nature and artifice, the gardens provide the serene backdrop necessary for contemplation and meditation, an alternative to the non-stop bustle of modern urban Japan. Some gardens also showcase rare plants or unusual rock forms; others were designed with recreation or strolling in mind. A strolling garden may be peppered with uneven surfaces, designed to bring the gaze down, then back up, to surprise the visitor—a manifestation of the Japanese design principle of "hide and reveal."

Gardens may feature water, islands, bridges, lanterns and teahouses. A great deal of symbolism goes into the design. Stones, for instance, which local legend holds to be infused with spirits, may embody mountains. Auspiciousness dictates they must be arranged in odd numbers and in triangular shapes. Lanterns and water are often put in proximity to represent the male-female, or yin-yang juxtaposition. Koi carp, with their associations of strength and perseverance, can sometimes be found in the pond. The technique of *shakkei*, or borrowed scenery, is used to harmonize the garden with its surroundings.

Garden scenes have been a mainstay of one of the most popular Japanese hobbies, embroidery and needlework. The techniques used date back more than a thousand years, and the fabrics created were originally used in religious ceremonies. The best embroidery involved silk, and the expense of the materials meant that such garments were traditionally the preserve of women of the court. However, it later filtered down to the general public as a result of necessity, as women adapted their clothes for the weather or aesthetic reasons. The costly and elaborate nature of kimono meant that they had to be kept in circulation in various reincarnations—a coat, jacket, vest, cushion cover, bags, and ultimately patchwork material—and sewing became a common skill, later undertaken for pleasure rather than need. Embroidered fabrics typically depict elements of nature such as flowers and gardens.

Right: Some Japanese cultural artifacts are highly ornate…

The perfect balance of nature and artifice,
Japanese gardens provide the serene backdrop
necessary for contemplation and meditation
and act as a remedy to the non-stop bustle of
modern Japan.

Below: … by contrast, flower
arranging
is all about simplicity
and linear harmony…

Similar precision is required in origami, the renowned Japanese art of paper-folding. Another Chinese import, the practice was initially confined to ceremonial uses, due to the high cost of paper. When paper became more affordable, origami was used as a form of children's entertainment, before the efforts of Akira Yoshizawa, the son of a dairy farmer who went on to become an origami grandmaster, stimulated a 20th century resurgence of interest and elevated the hobby. The crane is probably the flagship origami figure, and the Japanese have had plenty of encouragement to perfect the bird: it was said that once a person had made a thousand cranes, they would be granted one wish. The bird also symbolizes good luck and peace.

Origami is founded on the principles of mathematics and geometry. But while numbers feature in the latest craze to emerge from Japan, it is logic, not math, that is the key. Sudoku consists of a grid of nine by nine squares, containing nine smaller boxes of three by three squares. The grid must be completed with digits from one to nine, with the condition that the same digit must not be repeated in any row, column or three-by-three box. Depending on the placement of the initial numbers, the puzzle can be relatively easy or highly demanding, described by some Western newspapers that publish sudoku grids as "fiendish." A new version of the challenge plays on the Japanese connection: *samurai sudoku* fuses five grids together.

Above: An origami practitioner who makes a thousand cranes is said to be granted one wish.

Left: The carp, which swims against the tide, is a symbol of strength and perseverance.

But few people realize that the game was in fact invented not in Japan, but in Indianapolis, by an American architect named Howard Garns. Following low-key publication in the puzzle press, it was taken up by a Japanese publisher and renamed *sudoku*, a contraction of a Japanese phrase meaning "the digits can occur only once." In 2005 the puzzle became an international phenomenon, translating easily between cultures. Commuters around the world can often be seen pondering a sudoku grid on the train or bus home, and the second World Sudoku Championships were held in Prague, the Czech Republic, in 2007.

Below: Japanese gardens offer some respite from urban living.

Perhaps there is something in the Japanese psyche that makes the country prone to starting crazes. A few years before sudoku, it was *manga* that came to global prominence. Meaning "whimsical pictures," the word describes a kind of comic book story that betrayed strong Disney influences. Osamu Tezuka, the artist who pioneered modern manga after World War II, wrote stories whose only text was the dialogue spoken by the characters. Despite being written for children, some of the tales were rather dark. When Tezuka's readers grew up, they retained their enthusiasm for the genre, taking it mainstream, and manga now makes up a significant portion of the Japanese publishing industry. The dialogue-only format made manga easily adaptable for the screen, giving rise to *anime*, or animation. Of much greater importance in Japan than in the United States, anime styles and techniques have influenced animation around the world.

Such a synthesis and cultural borrowing is not visible in Japanese flower arranging, *ikebana*. Whereas Westerners prefer to accentuate colors and volume, in Japan this art is about linear harmony. The Japanese also attach more than just aesthetics: the final effort symbolizes heaven, earth, and humanity, again subscribing to the Japanese ideal of harmony between man and nature. The art developed from early ritualistic Buddhist offerings. In the 15th century, in line with the wishes of the ruling shogun Ashikaga Yoshimasa, an advocate of simplicity, the complicated rules of *ikebana* were made easier, opening up the art to the general public. Now a hobby and traditional art, once *ikebana* was an essential skill for a woman hoping to marry. The same was true of calligraphy. Both a way of communicating information and an art form in itself, this has remained a relatively exclusive interest.

Right: Bonsai, symbolizing the oneness of humankind and nature, developed from a practical necessity into an international art form.

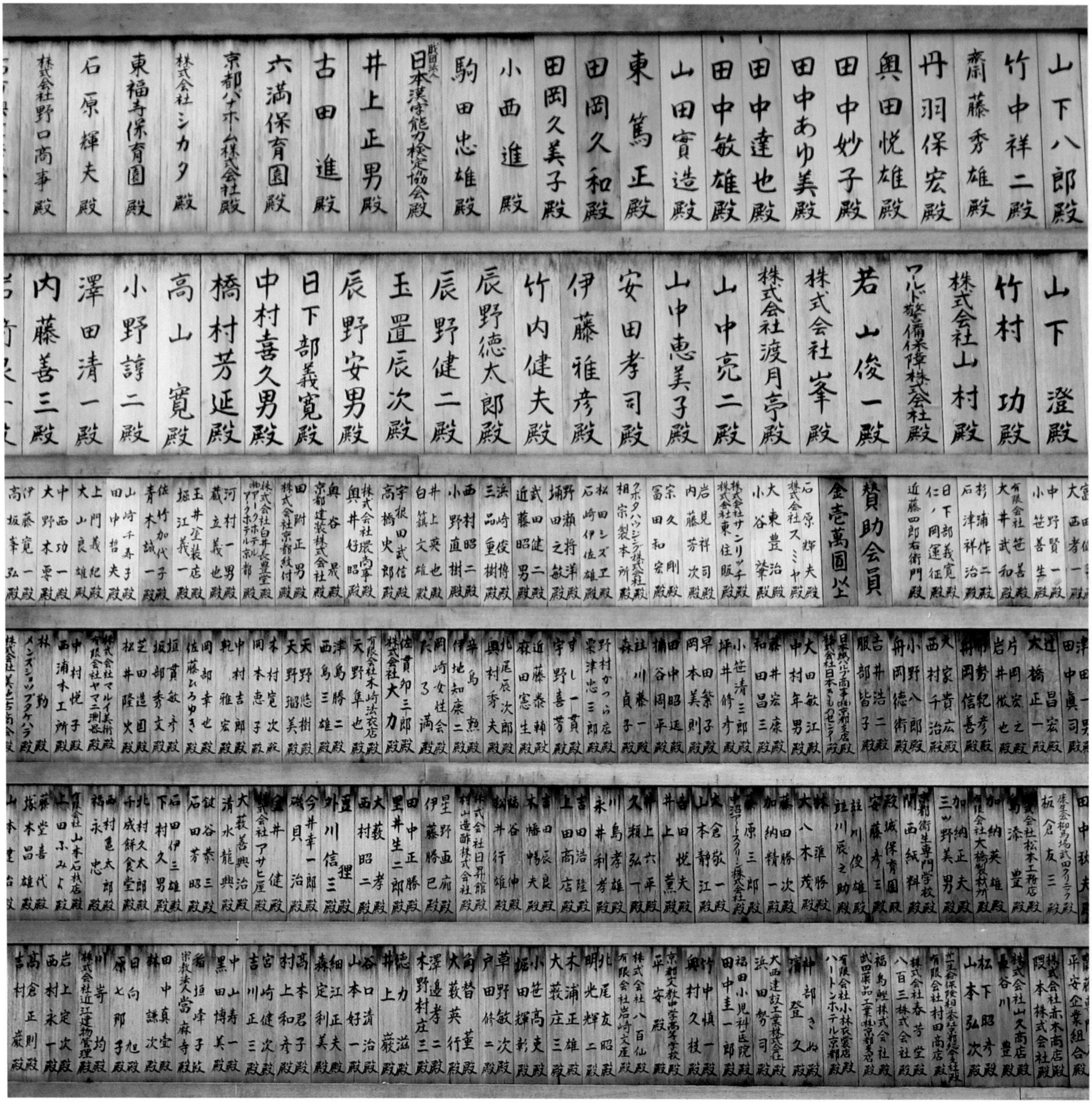
山下八郎殿
竹中祥二殿
齋藤秀雄殿
丹羽保宏殿
奥田悦雄殿
田中妙子殿
田中あゆ美殿
田中達也殿
田中敏雄殿
山田實造殿
東篤正殿
田岡久和殿
田岡久美子殿
小西進殿
駒田忠雄殿
財団法人日本漢字能力検定協会殿
井上正男殿
古田進殿
六満保育園殿
京都パナホーム株式会社殿
株式会社シカタ殿
東福寺保育園殿
石原輝夫殿
株式会社野口商事殿
山下澄殿
竹村功殿
株式会社山村殿
ワールド整備保障株式会社殿
若山俊一殿
株式会社峯殿
株式会社渡月亭殿
山中亮二殿
山中恵美子殿
安田孝司殿
伊藤雅彦殿
竹内健夫殿
辰野徳太郎殿
辰野健二殿
玉置辰次殿
辰野安男殿
日下部義寛殿
中村喜久男殿
橋村芳延殿
高山寛殿
小野諄二殿
澤田清一殿
内藤善三殿
賛助会員
金壱萬圓以上

Like several other aspects of Japanese culture, bonsai has its origins in China. Around 200 AD, the Chinese began to keep trees small by pruning and potting. One theory is that the method proved useful for moving the plants required for medicinal purposes from one place to another. These early techniques to preserve the plants' small stature remain in use. Contrary to what many believe, bonsai trees are not kept small by genetic manipulation, nor are they deprived of any essential nutrients. In fact a well-cared-for bonsai is likely to outlive a normal sized tree of its species, and some survive for centuries. In bonsai's infancy, the trees were comparatively large, and it is only in modern times that specimens have been produced at such small sizes, with the tiniest of all being potted in a container the size of a thimble.

From a practicality of transportation, the practice developed into an art, and early Chinese practitioners exhibited their trees in the form of various figures from mythology and the animal kingdom. The Heian Period, which ran from 794 to 1185, saw Japan borrow heavily from Chinese culture, and one of the customs that found their way across the water was bonsai, perhaps because it appealed to the delicate Japanese sense of style and aesthetics. Bonsai symbolizes the oneness of humankind and nature, and is also described as "heaven and earth in one container." To cultivate a tree in this way is a contemplative, meditative process, and it is easy to see why the tenets of Zen Buddhism are an important element of bonsai.

Much like tea, which was also introduced from China in the same period, bonsai was initially the preserve of the elite. But following the Chinese invasion of Japan in the 14th century, it became popularized among the masses, which possibly saved the practice from extinction. Bonsai came west in 1878, when samples were exhibited at the Third Universal Exhibition in Paris. Initially the bizarre-looking trees offended Western sensibilities and concepts of nature, but in time they came to be appreciated, with their popularity boosted by soldiers returning from Japan after World War II.

Above: Temples and shrines are among the country's most distinctive architecture.

Left: Despite the country's secularity, religious items and buildings are common sights in Japan.

Bonsai symbolizes the oneness of humankind and nature, and is also described as "heaven and earth in one container." To cultivate a tree in this way is a contemplative, meditative process.

Nowadays, aficionados can find collections in places as diverse as Brisbane, Australia; Marbella, Spain; Jakarta, Indonesia and Washington DC. Ironically, the majority of the trees that came over after the war, piquing outside interest in the practice, died, confirming one of the immutable truths of bonsai: they are notoriously hard for the uninitiated to keep alive.

Bonsai trees are not kept small by genetic manipulation, nor are they deprived of any essential nutrients. A well-cared-for bonsai is likely to outlive a normal-sized tree of its species, and some survive for centuries.

Left: Japanese gardens provide the ideal serene environment for the Buddhist practice of contemplation.

Right: Spirits are interwoven into the fabric of Japanese religion.

Shrines and Temples

The Japanese passion for harmony is also evident in the thousands of shrines and temples around the country. Many of these holy places in Japan are located near scenic natural surroundings or within immaculately planned and maintained gardens, which extend the area for quiet contemplation and spiritual thought beyond the walls of the temple buildings.

People visit shrines in order to pay respect to the *kami* (Shinto deities) or to pray for good fortune. Shrines are also visited during special events such as New Year and other festivals. Newborn babies are traditionally brought to a shrine a few days after birth, and many couples hold their wedding ceremonies at Shinto shrines. Funerals, however, are not generally held in Shinto shrines; nor are cemeteries located in the grounds of shrines, because according to Shinto belief, death is associated with impurity.

There are some traditional Japanese festivals celebrating children that are observed at Shinto shrines. One such children's festival is called *Shichi go san*, which means "seven five three." Girls of age three and seven and boys of age three and five are celebrated on *Shichi go san*, and families pray for their good health and growth. Each year on November 15 or the nearest weekend, parents dress their children in traditional kimono and take them to visit a Shinto shrine.

The earliest Shinto shrines in Japan were built to honor a particularly beautiful natural feature or place, such as a waterfall or large rock. Today, there are more than 85,000 Shinto shrines in Japan, ranging in size from small local shrines to large ones that are known throughout the nation. Shrines, called *jinja* in Japanese, are marked by an entrance gate called a *torii*. *Torii* have a distinctive shape, which consists in its most basic form of two horizontal pieces of wood with two vertical supports underneath. *Torii* are often painted dark orange or red, though the oldest ones are simply constructed of natural wood.

Visitors may walk through the *torii* and then along a tree-lined pathway up to the hall of worship. The shrine may contain one or two halls: the main hall, called a *honden*, houses the shrine's holy objects which are not to be viewed by the public. Only Shinto priests are allowed to enter the *honden*, which is the most sacred part of the shrine complex. The offering hall, or *haiden*, may be part of the same building as the *honden*, or it may be a separate building.

Shinto priests wear a black headdress and wide-legged trousers. Their outfit is completed by a robe with wide sleeves, in white for daily wear and black for special ceremonies. They wear traditional black wooden clogs. Shinto priests may be assisted in their duties by women who wear a red kimono with a white robe over the kimono.

Near the entrance to the shrine, visitors will find a purification fountain with several ladles. Visitors take a ladle, fill it with fresh water, and rinse their hands. Then they may put some water into a cupped hand, rinse their mouth, and spit the water out beside the fountain. In this purification ritual, the water is not supposed to be transferred directly from the ladle into the mouth, nor should it be swallowed. Visitors may also be asked to remove their shoes before entering the shrine.

Below: Torii *gates are often donated by worshippers in gratitude for their business success.*

The entrance to a shrine is typically guarded by two stone lions whose presence is said to ward off evil. One lion, with its mouth open, is called "a" (the first "letter" of the Japanese syllabic alphabet) and the other, depicted with its mouth closed, is called "un" (the last sound of the Japanese alphabet). Together, these two figures symbolize a baby's first cry and a person's last breath before dying—in other words, the beginning and end of life on earth.

At the entrance to the offering hall, visitors put one or several coins into the wooden collection box as offerings to the *kami*, or Shinto deities. There is usually a gong or bell for visitors to sound in order to attract the attention of the gods. Visitors then bow deeply twice, clap their hands twice to get the *kami*'s attention, bow deeply once more, and then pray for a few seconds.

Features of traditional Japanese architecture that can be found in the earliest shrines and temples, as well as early Japanese houses, include raised floors to help air circulation and low roofs extending over a veranda to protect the whole building from heavy rains. A low overhanging roof may be covered in thatch or tiles. Wood was the most common building material, as it was in plentiful supply and was flexible in earthquakes and breathed in humid environments. The interior and exterior are viewed together as a whole, and the use of sliding paper panels, called *shoji*, or movable screens creates partitions within the building or house.

Over the centuries, though, the architectural style and features of Shinto shrines and Buddhist temples have blended together. Only a few of today's shrines are considered to be built in a purely Japanese style. The most traditional and quintessentially Japanese shrines are Shinto's most important shrines, the Ise shrines.

Right: Silent contemplation— an elevated state in Japanese religion.

The architecture of Shinto shrines and Buddhist temples have blended, so very few remaining shrines are purely Japanese in style.

A pair of Ise shrines located near Nagoya are two of Shinto's most sacred shrines. The shrines are called Geku, the outer shrine which is dedicated to Toyouke, the *kami* of clothing, food and housing; and Naiku, the inner shrine. The inner shrine is believed to house the sacred mirror used by Amaterasu, the sun goddess. According to legend, the daughter of an emperor was traveling through Japan, looking for a place to keep the sacred mirror, when Amaterasu spoke to her and chose Ise as the site. In keeping with Shinto tradition, these Ise shrines are rebuilt every 20 years. An empty area of land is always left adjacent to each shrine as the site for the next

version. The next rebuilding of these shrines is expected to be in 2013. It is believed that Naiku was originally established in the 3rd century and Geku in the 5th century AD. These Ise shrines are also unusual in their extreme simplicity. The wooden shrine structures, including buildings, bridges, and gates, are barely painted, being instead left in their natural state. The grounds contain dense woods of green trees and broad gravel lanes. Unlike most other Shinto shrines, the Ise shrines are built in a purely Japanese architectural style which shows no influence from the Asian mainland.

Imperial shrines are another important category of Shinto shrines in Japan. These shrines were directly funded and administered by the Japanese government during the era when Shinto was fostered as the state religion, from 1868 until the end of World War II. Imperial shrines can be recognized by the imperial family's chrysanthemum crest. Meiji Shrine (called Meiji Jingu in Japanese) is a shrine in Tokyo dedicated to the deified spirits of Emperor Meiji and his consort, Empress Shoken. In the Shinto belief system, it is not uncommon to enshrine the deified spirits of important figures. Emperor Meiji was the first emperor of modern Japan, ascending to the position in 1868 when power was transferred from the feudal Tokugawa government to the imperial throne. The Meiji Shrine was completed in 1920, and was later rebuilt after being destroyed in World War II. It is located in a wooded area next to Yoyogi Park in Tokyo. Various events and festivals are celebrated at the Meiji Jingu shrine throughout the year.

Inari shrines are dedicated to Inari, the *kami*, or Shinto god, of rice. Inari shrines can be recognized by the fox statues near the entrance, rather than lion statues as in most Shinto shrines. The fox, called *kitsune* in Japanese, is considered to be the messenger of Inari. It is a common misconception that Inari is the "fox god."

Left: Japanese religious paraphernalia ranges from the ornate…

Below: … to the very simple.

Fushimi Inari Shrine, located near Kyoto, is the largest Inari shrine in Japan. It is famous for the countless red wooden *torii* ceremonial gates that line the hiking trails for pilgrims leading up the wooded mountain behind the shrine. These gates were donated by worshippers and companies in thanks for good luck or in hope of blessings. Pilgrims and other visitors can stop off at restaurants along the two-hour walk up the mountain to enjoy a bowl of *kitsune udon*, a noodle soup topped with pieces of fried tofu— which is said to be a favorite food of foxes.

Some powerful clans in Japanese history established and dedicated shrines to the their clans' founders. There are dozens of shrines, known as Toshogu shrines, which are dedicated to Tokugawa Ieyasu, the powerful 17th century *shogun* and founder of the Tokugawa shogunate, which ruled Japan for over 250 years until 1868. The Toshogu shrine at Nikko is the mausoleum of Tokugawa Ieyasu. The shrine is dedicated to the spirits of Ieyasu and two other influential figures from Japanese history, Toyotomi Hideyoshi and Minamoto Yoritomo.

The splendid Toshogu shrine complex consists of more than a dozen Shinto and Buddhist buildings set in a beautiful forest. Although Toshogu was originally constructed as a relatively simple mausoleum, it was enlarged and spectacularly embellished during the first half of the 17th century into the grand complex seen today by Ieyasu's grandson Iemitsu. In contrast to other typical shrines across Japan, where simplicity is stressed, Toshogu contains countless wood carvings and is lavishly decorated in large amounts of gold leaf. One of the most famous carvings depicts three monkeys in the "hear no evil, see no evil, speak no evil" gestures and is believed to be the source of this expression.

Left: Linear harmony and simplicity inform the principles of Japanese religious depictions.

Above: Religious iconography and buildings are designed to blend seamlessly with the natural elements.

Many traditional Japanese homes contain small altars, in the form of miniature shrines, to honor the *kami*, which are believed to be ever-present. Japanese people may place traditional offerings of sake and rice cakes in front of the altar before praying to the Shinto deities. Other objects with special spiritual significance, such as braided ropes and zigzag paper strips, may be draped on the altar. In modern-day Japan with its increasing secularization, however, fewer homes have these family altars.

Buddhism was introduced to Japan in the late 6th century, and its traditional temple architecture accompanied the faith from China and Korea. Japanese Shinto shrine architecture was also influenced by Chinese styles, with red paint beginning to be used on wooden columns of buildings and gates.

Nowadays nearly every city and town in Japan has at least one Buddhist temple complex. Kyoto is particularly renowned for its rich heritage in this area, boasting several thousand temples from humble structures to the fantastic Kinkaku-ji complex, with its exterior covered in real gold leaf.

Buddhist temple complexes contain several main structures. The most important are the main hall, where sacred objects such as statues are displayed; the lecture hall, which is used for worship and also for displaying sacred objects; and the pagoda, a tower usually with three or five tiered stories. Other elements of a typical Buddhist temple complex are the ornamental gate marking the entrance to the temple grounds, a large bell that is rung on ceremonial occasions, and a cemetery.

The main hall, or *hondo* in Japanese, contains an inner and an outer sanctuary. Worshippers gather in the outer part and face the inner sanctuary to pray. Statues and other images of the Buddha are located in the inner sanctuary. The main hall of Todai-ji, which means "Great Eastern Temple," in the city of Nara is the largest wooden building in the world today—despite the fact that the present building, constructed in 1692, is only two-thirds the size of the original hall. Todai-ji also claims another superlative: the main hall houses Japan's largest Buddha statue, or *daibutsu*.

There is usually a large incense bowl located in front of the *hondo*. Worshippers burn incense sticks and waft the smoke over their bodies to purify themselves.

The pagoda tower has its origins in the Indian *stupa*, originally a structure of veneration with symbolic meaning built to house sacred relics. To-ji temple in Kyoto is well-known for its five-story pagoda, which is Japan's tallest at 188 feet (57 m). Visitors are permitted to enter the pagoda at To-ji only a few days each year.

Buddhist temple complexes have a large bell made of iron or brass which is rung to mark the beginning of a ceremony. Each New Year's Eve, the bell is rung 108 times to ring in the new year and to banish the 108 worldly desires, according to Buddhist belief.

The huge temple bell at Kencho-ji has been designated a national treasure in Japan. It was cast in 1255. Kencho-ji is a magnificent Buddhist temple located in the city of Kamakura in the greater Tokyo area. Founded in 1253, Kencho-ji is one of the oldest Zen Buddhist temples in Japan and is considered to be the greatest of Kamakura's five Zen temples. The complex also contains a Buddhist monastery, where monks are trained for a life of contemplation.

Many Buddhist temple complexes are surrounded by magnificent gardens. Zen Buddhism is particularly associated with *karesansui*, or dry stone gardens. Rocks are central to the design of any Japanese garden, but this element is taken to the extreme in dry gardens. Japanese rock gardens use gravel and sand, raked into precise ridges and wavy patterns, to symbolize the movement of water. Zen gardens are places of contemplation and interpretation, often with symbolic meanings bound up in the arrangement of their elements and arrangements.

The rock garden at the Ryoan-ji temple in Kyoto, thought to have been built in the late 1400s, is the most famous Zen garden in Japan. It consists of nothing but 15 boulders, moss, and neatly raked gravel. The meaning of the garden's arrangement is left up to each visitor's interpretation. The 15 moss-covered boulders are placed so that when the garden is viewed from any viewpoint, only 14 of the boulders are visible at one time. It is traditionally said that only through attaining enlightenment—the ultimate aim of the Buddhist faith—would one be able to view the 15th boulder.

Right: By custom, visitors to sacred sites cleanse their hands and mouths.

Below: The ideal of conformity cuts across all aspects of Japanese life.

Many outdoor Buddhist statues that depict or are otherwise associated with children are dressed in bonnets and bibs or other garments to show that the parishioners of the temple are looking after them.

Mount Koya (*Koya-san* in Japanese), south of Osaka, is the center of a Buddhist sect known as Shingon Buddhism, which was introduced to Japan from China in the 9th century. There are over 100 temples at Koya-san, and about 50 of these offer overnight temple lodging, known as *shukubo*, to visiting tourists. Guests at temple lodgings are served *shojin ryori*, the vegetarian cuisine of monks, at mealtimes. At many *shukubo*, guests may also have the opportunity to participate in morning prayers, which typically start around 6 a.m. and last for about 30–45 minutes.

Some Buddhist temple complexes in Japan include *ryokan*, or traditional inns, similar in concept to bed-and-breakfasts. The *ryokan* at the Chikurin-in temple in the town of Yoshino, southwest of Tokyo, originally served as lodging for practitioners of a mountain-worshipping tradition. Nowadays, though, it is an extremely popular place for visitors to stay in the cherry blossom season each springtime.

Left: These lanterns have stood in their formation for many years.

Right: Snow lanterns are a less permanent decoration.

Nature and Nourishment

Outside its bustling cities, Japan boasts an endlessly fascinating display of flora and fauna. Its close relation with the sea is reflected in the nation's cuisine.

In Japan, gardens are considered an art form. Careful attention is paid to the arrangement of elements—not just plants, trees, and flowers, but rocks and water too. Some gardens are designed to be observed from one particular viewing point, such as a temple; others are laid out to offer a variety of vistas to visitors who stroll through along a carefully planned path. Gardens are often found adjoining temples or shrines, thereby becoming places of spirituality and contemplation. In all cases, the objective of Japanese garden design is to provide a harmonious whole through the judicious use of textures, colors, and materials.

Japanese gardens can be classified into three broad groups: *tsukiyama*, or hill gardens; *karesansui*, or rock gardens; and *chaniwa*, or tea ceremony gardens.

Tsukiyama gardens emphasize rolling scenery with small hills (often man-made), shrubs, trees, flowers, and ponds. All of these features are separated by broad lawns. Often bridges or small gazebos are placed in the garden to encourage visitors to view the garden from a particularly scenic angle.

Tsukiyama garden design was first developed in the 5th century AD. Many famous gardens recreate famous landscapes—such as mountains or coastlines, for example—in miniature. In fact, the word *tsukiyama* means "constructed mountain."

Perhaps Japan's most famous hill landscape garden is Kenrokuen, located in the grounds of Kanazawa Castle near the west cost of Honshu, Japan's main island. It contains many streams, waterfalls, and ponds, which are fed by a specially-constructed system of channels constructed in the 17th century to transport water from a distant river to the garden. Kenrokuen has been open to the public since the late 1800s, but before that, it was part of the private grounds surrounding the castle belonging to the ruling Maeda clan. The literal translation of the name Kenrokuen is "Garden of the Six Sublimities." This refers to six important qualities that successful gardens should contain, according to an ancient theory: spaciousness, seclusion, artificiality, antiquity, abundant water, and broad views.

Above: Plants are chosen for their suitability for their surroundings.

Left: For urban residents, parks and gardens are important as places for contemplation.

Above: A serene pond.

Right: Rice plants require a watery environment.

It may seem odd to Western sensibilities to use the term "garden" to refer to *karesansui*, or rock gardens. Whereas the essential element of a Western garden is vegetation of some sort, *karesansui* take a different, more abstract, approach. They recreate natural landscapes using rocks and stones of different sizes, gravel, and sand. Sometimes patches of moss are included to add contrasting texture and to symbolize islands or mountains.

Often intricate patterns will be made in a large area of sand or gravel with a rake or other implement to symbolize waves or rows of crops.

Of course visitors must not walk on these surfaces that have been groomed with such care.

Karesansui gardens are ideal places for quiet contemplation and meditation, and are often influenced by the principles of Zen Buddhism. The Zen temple of Ryoanji in Kyoto is famous for its rock garden. White gravel is raked into precise patterns around large rocks and moss. The exact symbolic meaning of the garden's arrangement is unknown; thus, visitors can gaze in contemplation in order to arrive at their own interpretation of the various elements and their interrelationships.

Chaniwa gardens date back to the 14th century. They take their name from the tradition-laden Japanese tea ceremony, as they are typically located adjacent to a tea house. The focus in *chaniwa* is the approach to the tea house and preparation for the elaborate tea ceremony which takes place within. Stepping stones lead up to the entrance of the tea house, and there is typically a stone fountain or basin where guests cleanse themselves prior to the tea ceremony. Stone lanterns are also a common feature. *Chaniwa* gardens are usually designed to be simple, in order to evoke feelings of calmness and serenity.

In all Japanese gardens, harmony in color is also generally preferred. For this reason, the emphasis is usually on green plants and trees, rather than flowers. When they are used, colorful displays of flowers are generally restricted to the entrance to a garden. Some trees, such as the Japanese maple or cherry, may be used to add seasonal bursts of color.

Because so much of Japan is mountainous, farmland is precious and scarce. Only about 14 percent of the nation's total area is suitable for cultivation. Even so, Japanese farmers have been able to use what farmland is available extremely effectively—particularly through the use of terraced fields, so that crop yields per acre (hectare) are very high. As a result, the country has been largely self-sufficient in terms of food throughout its history, even as Japan's population has grown. This is changing, however, with changing trends in eating habits. Past generations ate a diet based chiefly on rice, vegetables, and seafood. Younger Japanese are eating more meat and dairy products, most of which must be imported.

The status of rice as the central part of the traditional Japanese diet is mirrored in its importance as a cash crop. It is believed that rice plants were introduced into Japan sometime around the first century BC. Rice plants are very labor-intensive to grow, as they require carefully controlled water supplies. As rice cultivation became more sophisticated, Japanese farmers developed complex irrigation networks to provide their paddy fields with the necessary water around the growing plants. Japan does not have a monsoon season like other major rice-growing countries, so irrigation is needed. Nowadays, though, the backbreaking manual labor involved in transplanting rice seedlings has been superseded by modern agricultural machinery. Because of the small, often awkward sizes of terraced fields, Japanese tractors, combines, and other farm equipment tend to be smaller than those used on large farms in the United States and Canada.

Left: A single blossom floats on the water.

Below: Balance and harmony are important in Japanese garden design.

Other important agricultural products include grains such as barley; soybeans, which are made into tofu and soy sauce, among other foodstuffs; some fruit and vegetables; and legumes. Japan must import more and more wheat as its population's preferences shift to include more bread—in sandwiches and hamburgers especially.

Livestock as a source of meat has never been a really important part of Japanese agriculture, since Japanese people generally prefer other sources of protein, such as fish and bean-based products. One exception, however, is Kobe beef, named after the region where the black breed of cattle that produce this premium type of meat are raised. Kobe beef is prized all over the world for its flavor, tenderness, and well-marbled fat. Farmers believe that the care of the cattle is important for the quality of the meat, and Kobe cattle enjoy lives of real luxury—they are even treated to massages, as this is thought to improve the marbling!

Left: A Japanese maple tree provides a mass of color.

Below: Some maples have leaves that are red all year round.

Some plant products from Japan find uses other than as foodstuffs. One particularly versatile plant is bamboo. Although it can be quite woody and tough, bamboo is technically classified as a member of the grass family. A true renewable resource, some varieties of bamboo can grow as much as three feet (1 m) per day! Bamboo grows wild in Japan, but it is also cultivated as a cash crop. Bamboo plants spread by sending out runners under the ground. While this characteristic can be undesirable in a garden, it has a particular benefit in an earthquake-prone place like Japan. The dense underground network of roots and runners produced by a bamboo grove or plantation makes the surface of the soil hold together, which means that a bamboo grove is quite a safe place to be during an earthquake!

Bamboo has been used in a multitude of applications since prehistoric times. When bamboo stems are treated, they become tough and woody and can be used as structural elements in furniture, scaffolding, fences, houses, and even as reinforcing rods in concrete. Other practical items that can be made from bamboo are walking sticks, kitchen utensils, musical instruments, and toys. Bamboo can be carved into ornamental objects. Because mature bamboo stems are hollow, they can be used as pipes to transport water. Japanese gardens may feature small waterfalls created by water flowing from the end of a carefully placed bamboo tube into a pond. And of course, the tender young shoots of the bamboo plant can be eaten, too.

More than two-thirds of Japan's land area is covered by forests. The northern island of Hokkaido, with its cold winters, features large

numbers of coniferous forests, particularly fir and spruce. The temperate regions include a mixture of deciduous trees, such as maple, beech, birch, oak, and ash, and conifers. Cypress, firs, and cedars are the main coniferous trees found in Japanese temperate forests. This mixture of deciduous trees and conifers produces breathtaking displays of autumn color to rival the finest New England fall foliage. To the south, in the subtropical regions such as Shikoku island, broadleaf evergreen species such as evergreen oak and laurel can be found.

The Japanese maple tree, a native of the island nation, is widely favored as a feature in Japanese gardens. Its overall shape when mature is generally dome-like, and its leaves have very long, narrow, pointed lobes. The Japanese maple is famed for its deep red autumn color, which can serve as a dramatic focal point in a carefully planned garden.

It is probably not surprising that many Japanese people enjoy getting away from the densely populated urban areas to take part in outdoor activities like hiking in the woods and mountains or visiting peaceful gardens. In the summertime, higher mountain elevations can also provide welcome relief from the sweltering heat of the cities. In the winter, weekend ski trips are popular. As a result of Japan's rapid urbanization after World War II, the countryside was rapidly depopulated. During school vacations and holiday periods, many scenic sites can get very busy, so that a trip to the mountains or the woods or Zen garden might not provide as much relaxation as one would hope.

Above: Hollow bamboo has a range of uses.

Right: Items made from bamboo are very durable.

Left: Bamboo plants will spread easily.

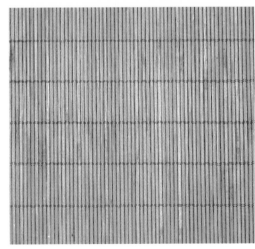

Animals of Japan

Thanks to its isolated geographical position, Japan has a number of animal species all its own.

One charming inhabitant of the forest is the Japanese macaque, also known as the snow monkey. A native of northern Japan, the macaque is actually the most northern-living of all the primates—other than humans, of course. Japanese macaques have brownish-gray fur and reddish-pink faces and paws. They have short tails.

Macaques find their food in the forests where they live. Berries, seeds, tender young plant shoots, fungi, even birds' eggs and small invertebrates make up their diverse diet. Like raccoons (and humans too), macaques wash their food before eating it.

Japanese macaques are affectionate and playful in their groups, or "troops," which can number anywhere between 20–100 individuals. Females usually outnumber males in a troop by about 3 to 1. They generally give birth to only one baby at a time. Macaques can live for up to 30 years in the wild.

Living as they do in regions with harsh winters, Japanese macaques are clever enough to take advantage of the many natural hot springs in their environment. Like little furry visitors to a luxury spa, they love to laze around in the warm water, happy to ignore the snow and ice all around. In the mountainous area around Nagano in central Honshu, people enjoy watching the macaques as they make their visits to bathe in the steamy natural pools.

The Buddhist faith has many legends involving macaques and other types of monkeys, and it is thought that the familiar maxim, "See no evil, hear no evil, speak no evil," may have originally been inspired by the antics of monkeys. Unlike in Western cultures, monkeys are a symbol of wisdom in Japan.

Appropriately enough for an island nation, Japan has an abundance of bird life. Ducks, geese, and swans are common on inland waterways. Other water birds such as herons and cranes are frequent sights too. Cranes are large, long-legged birds that breed on wetlands and feed on leaves, roots, insects, and even small animals. Images of cranes are familiar to aficionados of *origami*, the Japanese art of paper folding. Even novice paper-folders can easily master the basic form of the crane, with its long neck, small head, and large wings. Even though the crane is perhaps the best known bird of Japan, it is not the nation's official bird: that honor has been given to the Japanese pheasant, also known as the green pheasant. The Japanese pheasant is closely related to the common pheasant, but the males are distinguished by dark blue-green breast feathers.

Right: The crane's long legs help it wade through the water.

Below: The Japanese macaque spends most of its time in the forest.

Above: Japanese sika deer no longer have natural predators.

Right: Foxes appear in many ancient Japanese legends.

The sika deer is a close relative of the red deer and the North American elk (wapiti). It can be found in Siberia, Taiwan, Korea, and parts of China as well as Japan. As a result of geographical isolation, there is some variation among different populations of sika deer. The deer living on Hokkaido in the north tend to be larger than their cousins farther south.

In past centuries, sika deer were regarded as sacred in Japan. Later, when more people began to settle on Hokkaido, the deer were hunted almost to the point of extinction on that island. After the introduction of legislation in the early 20th century to protect them, the population rapidly recovered. Nowadays they wander among temple buildings in many places throughout Japan. They become tame easily, and tourists can photograph and even feed these deer.

There are two types of red fox native to Japan: the Hokkaido fox and the Japanese red fox. Like other Japanese animals, it migrated to Japan millennia

ago when there was a land connection between Japan and the rest of Asia. The red fox lives in many different habitats all over Japan, and it has adapted well to coexist with humans.

The ban-ei horse is a breed native to Japan. It is primarily used in racing, but unlike the sleek, streamlined horses that jockeys ride around race courses, the ban-ei has a stocky build. It was developed to be sturdy because the type of races it competes in involve pulling heavy weighted sleighs—with a jockey riding on top—along a straight track made of sand. As you might imagine, the pace of ban-ei races is a whole lot slower than that at the Kentucky Derby! Even so, people do place bets on the races. Ban-ei horse races are probably the only horse races where the jockeys could get off and walk alongside the horses, with no difficulty keeping up.

In the remoter parts of Hokkaido, the Asiatic black bear forages in the forests. The black bear is omnivorous, so its diet includes meat and

fish as well as berries and other plant material. Hunting of the black bear is strictly controlled by law in Japan. For centuries, the black bear has played a role in the traditional stories and tales of the indigenous Ainu people of Hokkaido.

Some animals native to Japan are extremely rare. The Iriomote cat, named for the small southern island near Okinawa where it lives, is called a "living fossil" because scientists believe it has changed very little from its primitive form. The Iriomote cat is approximately the same size as a house cat and has grayish-brown fur with darker spotted markings. It is extremely threatened as a species, with probably fewer than 100 individuals surviving. The main cause of its population decline has been the destruction of its habitat, though it is now protected by law.

The Japanese crested ibis, with its white plumage and striking red face, was once a very common bird in Japan. Its natural habitat is wetlands, and its diet consists mainly of frogs and small fish. Because of the continual loss of its habitat, though, the wild crested ibis was completely wiped out in Japan. For a time, it was thought that they were also extinct in China, but then a small population was discovered there. Now scientists are working to breed the species, which is classified as endangered.

Many animals, including the wolf, fox, and snake, as well as mythical creatures such as the dragon, are represented in traditional Japanese myths and folk tales. Many of these animals have characteristics that are very different from their Western counterparts. For example, the wolf is often presented as a benign creature. The fox spirit, often known as *kitsune*, is present in many Japanese tales. It is usually an intelligent creature, often with the ability to change into a human form. Foxes in Japanese stories may have several tails—even as many as nine—and the more tails the mythical fox has, the older, wiser, and cleverer it is. Modern Japanese tales, in the form of *manga* or comic-book novels aimed at adults, sometimes incorporate anthropomorphized animal characters.

In addition to wild animals and mythical creatures, the Japanese love pets just as much as we do. For city dwellers in densely populated urban areas, though, it is not always feasible to keep a large dog or other pet that needs its exercise. This lack of space was a decisive factor in the Japanese development of electronic and robotic toy "pets," which provide entertainment for their owners without the inconvenient aspects of real, live pets.

Food and Drink

Several countries can claim a strong affinity with tea. The Chinese, Indians, and British all cite their relationship with the beverage as a defining part of the national character. But it is the Japanese for whom tea is wound tightly into their philosophy, religion, politics, and culture.

They certainly cannot claim to have discovered it. It is believed that tea had been enjoyed in China for a millennium before it made its way across the sea in the 9th century. The man said to have brought it was a Buddhist monk called Eichu in the form of a kind of teacake. Legend has it that upon returning from China, where he had gone to study, Eichu made tea for the Emperor Saga. With the royal nod of approval, an official tea garden was established in the Imperial Palace, and the drink soon gained popularity among the noble and religious elite. It is interesting that the beverage's "early adopters" were an entirely different social class than one might imagine. Today, tea is a drink of the people. The Japanese use the metaphor *nichijo-sahan-ji*, which translates to "an everyday tea-meal affair," or ordinary event. But for the first few centuries of its development, the consumers were drawn exclusively from the top stratum of society. Today's tea drinker would probably not have enjoyed the infusion, which was seasoned with salt.

Religious figures in particular paid attention to tea. It was another monk, Eisai, who brought over a new brew from China in the 12th century, reviving the drink after a drop in popularity following the cooling of Japan's relations with its large neighbor. This new product was a powdered green tea, with which Japan is now synonymous. The monks were particularly impressed by the capacity of the beverage, full of vitamins and minerals, to prevent sleepiness and enable the drinker to remain alert for long periods of meditation. Eisai was such a fan that he wrote a two-volume book, *Kissa-yojo-ki*, or *Tea Drinking for the Cultivation of Life*, at the end of the 12th century, in which he asserted that the beverage could help people live longer. "Tea is the ultimate mental and medical remedy and has the ability to make one's life more full and complete," began the tome, going on to explain how the drink helped the organs, in particular the heart, reduced the effects of alcohol (something which endeared it to Minamoto no Sanetomo, the third shogun, known for his excessive alcohol consumption), plus myriad other benefits.

Eisai also introduced Zen Buddhism to Japan, and creed and drink became inextricably entwined. Devotees would offer tea to the Buddha, then drink some themselves. The samurai, Japan's warrior caste, soon found that the contemplative aspects of Zen were in accord with their own principles and outlook, and started to make and drink green tea. This heralded the start of the tea ceremony, or *chanoyu*, which translates as "hot water for tea."

Right: "Tea is the ultimate mental and medical remedy and has the ability to make one's life more full and complete," wrote Eisai.

Below: Tea was bound up in the ethos of Zen Buddhism.

Chanoyu has no equivalent in any other culture. Part get-together, part art form, part spiritual expression; it is difficult for an outsider to reconcile the highly complex aspects of the tea ceremony with something as everyday as drinking tea, without understanding the Japanese psyche. The tea ceremony has an aesthetic simplicity, and embodies the Zen traits of harmony, respect, devotion, purity, and tranquility, all very Japanese ideals. It was not just a case of pouring tea. Knowledge of flower-arranging, calligraphy, kimono, ceramics, and incense must all be acquired before one could host a tea ceremony—even to attend as a guest you must know how to behave and what to do. Lafcadio Hearn, the Greek-born author who wrote extensively on Japan, noted, "The tea ceremony requires years of training and practice… yet the whole of this art, as to its detail, signifies no more than the making and serving of a cup of tea. The supremely important matter is that the act be performed in the most perfect, most polite, most graceful, most charming manner possible."

For centuries tea remained the drink of the elite. But from the 14th to 16th century, two new phenomena brought tea to the masses. One was the increasing popularity of tea gatherings, local get-togethers where the participants would take part in an early form of taste-testing: sampling the tea and trying to guess where it was from. Entrepreneurs also had a role, beginning to sell the drink to worshippers at religious sites.

Left: The tea ceremony embodies the Zen traits of harmony, respect, devotion, purity, and tranquility.

Below: "The supremely important matter is that the act be performed in the most perfect, most polite, most graceful, most charming manner possible."

Right: Sharing sake is a social gesture, and drinking from someone else's cup a sign of friendship and honor.

Below: Sake has come a long way since it was fermented by chewing in the mouth.

Sake, or rice wine, is produced through a process of multiple fermentation—like beer.

Re-established dealings with China, new technology and Japan's transformation from feudal land to modern society all influenced the development of tea, both in terms of production technology and also what the new Japanese preferred to drink. Relations with China, responsible for such a large part of Japan's tea-drinking culture, and citizens' attitude to their own feudal past saw the teas and ceremonies associated with each wax and wane. But despite variations in form, the ceremony remains a distinctive and significant part of the nation's culture. It has informed aspects of Japan's art, architecture, and religion. And all thanks to the humblest of beverages.

Given the significance of rice in Asian culture, it is hardly surprising that Japan's national drink has rice as its base. What is more surprising, at least to an outsider, is that rice wine, as we think of *sake*, in fact bears more resemblance to beer, being produced through a process of multiple fermentation. Steamed rice is fermented with a type of mold and water. But while the method might not sound particularly appealing, it is certainly preferable to the traditional way.

Exactly how *sake* originated is undocumented. One theory has it that the idea was borrowed from the Chinese, who started brewing rice along the Yangtze River almost 5,000 years BC. Another holds that the drink was a happy accident, a byproduct of wet rice fermentation, which started in Japan in the 3rd century. But what's for sure is that the first example was *kuchikami no sake*, literally "chewing in the mouth sake." Villagers were required to chomp on a mixture of rice, acorn, chestnuts, and grain—and then simply spit it out. Enzymes present in the saliva turned the starch to sugar, which would be left to ferment with grain. The spitting method persisted for centuries, until the discovery that *koji* could do the job better, a technique now used in soy sauce production.

In time the drink came to the attention of the Imperial Palace in Kyoto, which set up a brewing organization and employed full-time brewers. With royal money behind it, the technology quickly improved—the Japanese were using pasteurization for the purpose five centuries before Pasteur gave his name to it. In the second half of the 19th century, the law allowed anyone to set up a sake brewery, but the fillip in their number was soon ended by high taxation. Two wars also hindered the drink's development. Aiming to boost its war coffers by getting the public to buy highly taxed sake, the government banned homebrew during the Russo-Japanese War, at the start of the 20th century. During World War II, rice could not be spared for sake. Although production and quality went up after the war, by this time beer was surpassing the Japanese drink in popularity.

Despite this, it retains its cultural importance. Not only is it used in Shinto purification rituals and to celebrate big sports victories and the New Year, it was also the drink of choice for the kamikaze pilots of World War II to steel their nerves for their deadly missions.

To drink sake, which can be served hot or cold depending on season, type and preference, the Japanese way, it's customary for companions to pour each other's share. To drink from another's cup is a sign of friendship.

Of all Japanese cuisine, the iconic food is sushi, bringing, as it does, the aesthetics of Japanese simplicity of design to the table—or even the conveyor belt. Whereas many aspects of the country's culture started among the nobles and gradually filtered down to the masses, sushi took the opposite trajectory. It started out as a filler for the working class, a cheap stall food. Sushi was based on a technique that had been discovered in southeast Asia around 500 BC, when it was realized that cooked rice would ferment, and any fish that was packed in it would be preserved. It was over a thousand years before the concept reached Japan, and more than another thousand before sushi developed into its modern form—raw fish on rice with vinegar. Until the 15th century the rice had been discarded, but from then on the Japanese took a less wasteful attitude, consuming both fish and rice.

It was 1824 when a Tokyo entrepreneur called Yohei Hanaya pioneered the practice of shaping the rice by hand before adding a small piece of raw fish on the top. The owner of a food stall, Hanaya is said to have developed the method to placate rushed customers who did not want to wait for him to use a box, which was the standard technique of the time. Raw sushi was popularized about a hundred years later, when the Japanese started to use refrigerators. The food had a brief hiatus after World War II, when the Americans decided that the street stalls were unsanitary and banned them. Since then it has exploded in popularity. From its humble beginnings, sushi soon became an expensive delicacy. Its transformation from fast food for the masses to high-class gastronomy is neatly summed up by the story of tuna. The fatty belly-meat of bluefin tuna, known as *otoro* and *shimofuri*, was used as cat food until the 1950s. A shortage of tuna—caused, it is believed, by the testing of nuclear weapons in the Pacific Ocean—prompted the Japanese government to run a marketing campaign to reposition the fish. It is now the most expensive cut of tuna, with a small piece commonly costing around $10 in a restaurant. And don't expect to be able to take your time over the portion. In the late 1950s, restaurateur Yoshiaki Shiraishi removed the chairs and installed a conveyor belt in his eatery to minimize turnaround time. The concept took off, and as a result diners can be in and out in just 12 minutes.

Above: From its humble beginnings as fast food for the masses, sushi has become high-class gastronomy.

Left: Sushi brings the aesthetics of Japanese simplicity of design to the table.

Delicate, exquisite presentation is evident throughout Japanese cuisine. Its aesthetic was also shaped by the traditions of the common people.

Sushi is based on a technique that was discovered in Southeast Asia around 500 BC.

Below: Small portions, which initially developed from poverty, are one factor in Japanese longevity.

Sushi's delicateness and exquisite presentation is evident throughout Japanese cuisine, the aesthetic of which was also shaped by the traditions of the common people. Lack of money meant that the typical Japanese could not afford to buy large quantities of an ingredient, so they would eat from several small dishes. In keeping with the nation's ideas about being in harmony with nature and simplicity, much of the food is seasonal and based on combinations of staples, like rice or noodles, with fish or meat, vegetables or tofu. Flavoring comes from a high salt content, *dashi*, which is a seaweed stock, *miso*, fermented rice, barley and soybeans, rice wine, rice vinegar, and soy sauce, which has now come into use the world over.

Soy is one of the essential elements of Japanese cuisine. Soybeans have been farmed in China for three millennia, but nobody thought to experiment by making a sauce until the 3rd century BC. The idea reached Japan by way of a monk returning from China. Indeed, one of the reasons for the popularity of soy sauce was its lack of meat-based ingredients, which complied with the Buddhist doctrine of vegetarianism. So much did Japan's Buddhist clergy embrace the idea that in the early days soybean farming was mostly carried out by the priests themselves. The fermentation process eventually yielded two distinct products, *miso* and soy sauce, and as peace gradually settled over Japan, the samurai, whose martial skills were no longer in such high demand, moved into *miso* production.

Even more than soy, though, Japanese cuisine is built on rice. So integral is the foodstuff to the national cuisine, that *gohan*, which means "cooked rice," is also the word for a meal. From its introduction by way of Korea and Japan in the first century AD, the rice industry became the backbone of society, fiscal and political as much as gastronomical. Farms were taxed on rice production, which drove feudal lords into battle with each other, everyone trying to increase his share of Japan's limited supply of suitable farmland. Farmers enjoyed high social status, above merchants and servants, and second only to the ruling samurai. At that time, rice played an equivalent role to gold in Europe: a basic economic unit.

But the rice industry changed appreciably following shortages after World War II. Land reforms saw plots taken from anyone who was not using them to produce food, and given to tenant farmers. As farming declined in prestige and profit, trading—once seen as inferior to working the land—was eclipsing it, and the rural young headed to the city to seek work in manufacturing. Once the heart of the economy, rice production is now subsidized by the government. But while its glory days as a financial mainstay may be gone, its importance in the diet and culture of the Japanese people remains.

Above: Upscale Japanese cuisine has been embraced throughout the Western world.

Right: Noodles made from wheat are an alternative to rice.

Due to Japan's island geography, another culinary foundation is fish, with the Buddhist no-meat policy also increasing the prominence of seafood in the national diet. While Western culture, business, and foodstuffs have infiltrated Japan, with young people increasingly tempted by burgers and fast food, seafood remains the top dish, and government research has found that households spend more on it than any other food. Fish is ubiquitous: in sushi bars, business meetings—Japan even has fish hotdogs. And the Japanese love of ritual and symbolism means that much of it is imbued with significance. A winning sumo wrestler is rewarded with sea bream. Carp, the fish that swims against the river, is associated with perseverance and strength. This high regard for the breed sees ornamental carp showcased in fish ponds and a popular baseball team called the Hiroshima Carp. Seafood is also thought to be of practical benefit. Kelp, or seaweed, is believed to help keep women's hair black, and when scientists found evidence that fish eyeballs were rich in a fatty acid that is said to boost brain function, cramming students sent demand soaring.

Left above: Delicacy of presentation is a priority for the island nation.

Left below: Government research has found that Japanese households spend more money on fish than any other food.

Far left: Seafood has resisted challenges from Western cuisine to remain Japan's favorite food.

Above: Desserts are a lesser-known element of Japanese cuisine.

Right: Teppanyaki, hugely popular across several continents, turns cooking into something more akin to performance art.

While the case for blacker hair and higher grades may not be proven, Japanese cuisine is undoubtedly one of the world's healthiest. The country enjoys the highest life expectancy in the world, thanks in part to its low-fat, low-cholesterol, low-meat diet. Smaller portions with a wait between courses, which is a common way to take meals, results in better digestion. Portions are often cooked in different ways and include different ingredients, which encourages moderation. The island of Okinawa was a health phenomenon even within Japan, where residents' low-salt, low-sugar and high-vegetable intake had them living even longer than their compatriots. But while healthy diets traditionally suggest tastelessness and boring

abstemiousness, Japan's gastronomy is alive with vibrant tastes like *wasabi*, or Japanese horseradish.

And the health benefits can only be helped by the convivial style in which Japanese meals are taken. Many dishes are shared, and if you're drinking with your meal, the custom is to serve other diners, rather than yourself, and they will serve you. You will likely sit on cushions around low tables, creating an intimate atmosphere. Meals start with the phrase *itadakimasu*, a form of grace that means "I gratefully receive," and conclude with *gochisosama* (*deshita*), which expresses your thanks for the meal.

Strictly Business

Japan emerged from the aftermath of World War II to claim its place as a global economic superpower. Its high-tech innovations have set the pace for progress around the world.

In the film *Back to the Future Part III*, a 1980s teenager travels back in time to 1955 where he befriends an eccentric scientist, Dr. Brown. The movie includes lots of gags based on the difference between 1950s and modern-day America. In one exchange, when the pair are fixing a power circuit, the doctor remarks, "No wonder this circuit failed; it says 'Made in Japan.'" The teen replies, "What do you mean, Doc? All the best stuff is made in Japan." Looking shocked, Brown pronounces this state of affairs "unbelievable."

The scene neatly illustrates the incredible revolution undergone by the reputation and quality of Japanese industry. While someone from the 1950s equates Japanese technology with faultiness, a young person now cannot remember a time when it was not synonymous with quality. In the United States, there is an urban myth that the Japanese town of Usa on Kyushu Island was so named to allow local companies to circumvent their nation's poor industrial standing by marking imports "Made in USA." Of course the fact that Usa's history predates the United States' existence by centuries gives the lie to the story.

Dr. Brown would doubtless have been astonished to hear that in 2000 Japan became the largest car-producing country in the world, and that in 2007 its top brand Toyota was expected to overtake General Motors to become the number one automobile company in the world. Much of this success has been spurred by war. In the lead-up to World War II, increased demand for trucks led many Japanese automobile firms—whose typical practice was to produce cars in partnership with a European carmaker—to design their own vehicles for the first time. The United States was still occupying Japan at the start of the 1950s, and as a result commissioned trucks for use in the Korean War, laying the foundations for the boom of the Japanese car industry in the 1960s. But cars were not the only business booming at that time. United States investment and local government interventionism helped foster the Japanese post-war economic miracle, along with unprecedented levels of industry cooperation, big bank loans, and strong unions.

The postwar boom period had left Japan with strong iron and steel firms, a flexible and forward-thinking automobile industry, and an impressive manufacturing sector that managed to thrive despite the island's relative lack of natural resources. Besides rice and fish, little else could be naturally encouraged. So the country turned to the one thing that it was not lacking: innovation.

One area in which Japan has been a global leader is in transportation systems—particularly its high-speed "bullet" trains, which are known as *shinkansen* in Japanese. The name means "new trunk line" and refers to the special tracks which had to be laid parallel to existing rail lines to accommodate the high-speed trains. Thanks to their streamlined design and particularly long sections of track (which help to make the rails as seamless as possible), these hi-tech trains operate at speeds well above 150 mph (240 km/h). At such high speeds, safety is an important consideration. *Shinkansen* trains have an excellent safety record. Special sensors can detect an earthquake which might dislodge the rails from their proper position and bring the train to a halt very quickly. The high-speed railway lines pass through many specially-constructed tunnels and along bridges and viaducts, thereby avoiding level road crossings for reasons of safety.

Above: In a blur of motion, a train arrives at the station platform.

Left: The bullet train's streamlined design helps it attain astonishing speeds.

Japan has been a global leader in transportation systems—particularly its high-speed "bullet" trains, which are known as *shinkansen* in Japanese.

The *shinkansen* trains are electric, drawing their power from overhead lines. Comprising up to 16 cars, a *shinkansen* train can accommodate 1,000 passengers or more. The cars offer comfort and convenience to passengers on board, with first-class sections offering even greater luxury. Some trains feature double-decker cars, and while there are no restaurant cars on the *shinkansen*, passengers who cannot make it through their entire journey without some form of sustenance can purchase snacks on board.

The Japanese railway network has its origins back in the 19th century, however. Most of the engineers and workers involved in the construction of the first railway line were from Europe. One legacy of the early British involvement in Japan's railways is the fact that even today, Japanese trains always run on the left-hand track. In fact, cars in Japan drive on the left too, just as in Britain.

The first railway line in Japan opened in 1872 between Yokohama and Shimbashi, now part of Tokyo. It took 35 minutes to travel the 18-mile (29 km) distance between the end stations. Passenger services were the first to be introduced on this line, with freight trains coming later.

By 1987, the government-owned Japanese National Railways (JNR) was deep in debt as a result of heavy borrowing to finance its capital projects. That year the Japanese Diet (parliament) privatized the JNR, splitting it into several private companies which are now all part of the Japan Railways Group.

There are currently six main *shinkansen* lines on the islands of Honshu and Kyushu, with more planned and under construction. The first line, known as the Tokaido Line, was opened in 1964 between Tokyo and Osaka, in time to carry visitors to the Summer Olympics in Tokyo that year. Nowadays the trip between these two cities, a distance of some 350 miles (560 km), takes just two and a half hours. Even though French TGV trains are faster on average than the *shinkansen*, the TGV cannot compare with the Japanese high-speed network in terms of passenger numbers and frequency of trains.

Left: Japanese companies are among the most modern and innovative in the world.

Above: Telecommunications played a big part in the 1980s boom in the land of the rising sun.

Above: In today's economy, global links are important.

If passengers happen to miss one train, they can count on another one to come along in just seven to ten minutes during rush hours. Japanese trains are famed for their punctuality—so much so that lateness is measured not in minutes, but in seconds! According to recent statistics, the average "lateness" for *shinkansen* trains on the Tokyo line was 12 seconds. By the time the Tokaido Line celebrated its 40th anniversary in 2004, over 4 billion passenger journeys had been completed on that line alone.

But the progress of the super-fast Japanese railways does not stop with the *shinkansen*—current

research into maglev (magnetic levitation) train systems, which use powerful electromagnetic fields to "levitate" trains slightly above the rails, thereby reducing friction on the wheels, indicates that the journey time between Tokyo and Osaka could be cut to just an hour.

With such large numbers of people needing to get to and from work and school in a densely populated country, local mass transit systems are also important in Japan. Besides Tokyo, the cities of Fukuoka, Kobe, Kyoto, Nagoya, Osaka, Sapporo, Sendai, and Yokohama all have their own subway systems. Other cities around Japan, including Chiba,

Kamakura, Kitakyushu, and Naha (in Okinawa prefecture) have monorail systems, and still others have tram networks.

Tokyo's underground train system is actually a combination of two networks operated by different companies, though holders of pre-paid passes can use both networks.

Like most underground subway networks around the world, each line on the Tokyo system is assigned a color, so visitors who cannot read the Japanese names can still navigate their way around the system. The Ginza line, which opened in 1927, was the first subway line in all of Asia.

Like the *shinkansen* trains, the Tokyo subway trains are frequent and punctual, and they carry a huge number of passengers each day. Well over 200,000 passengers pass through some of the stations in central Tokyo each weekday. Because the subway trains can get extremely crowded, passengers often have to push their way into the cars. But despite the occasional discomfort of having to stand on a jam-packed train or subway car, Japanese rail transport is extremely effective at getting millions of busy people to their destinations.

Below: Japan is a leader in high-tech electronic consumer gadgets.

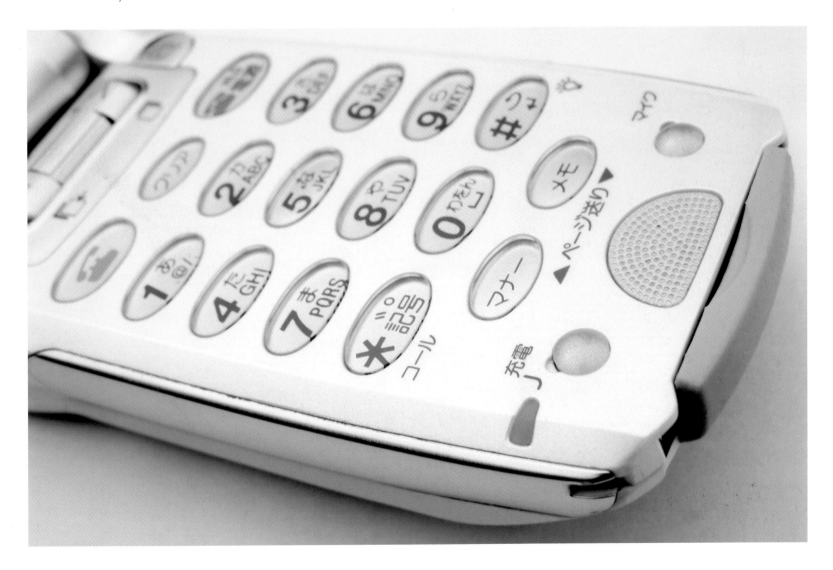

The Japanese consumer electronics industry is also a global leader. There can be few people who watch television, record a favorite program, listen to music, or type on a computer who have not used Japanese technology to do it, thanks to the country's success in exporting its products. The big names—such as Sony, Panasonic, Hitachi, Fujitsu, NEC, Toshiba, Canon, Mitsubishi, Sharp, Sanyo, JVC, and TDK—are among the best known and most trusted in their field, globally. Some commentators attribute the reliability and consistency of their output to the social organization of the country and working culture, which generally encourages uniformity and meticulousness. But the industry's dominance was also a natural follow-on from the products it had excelled in making in earlier years, the transistor of the 1950s followed by improving semiconductors in subsequent decades. These were typically made by big, integrated companies, who forged ahead through cost-cutting and miniaturization. It is little surprise that the product that perhaps exemplifies the trend of making things smaller was the Sony Walkman, the precursor of today's iPod.

Whatever consumer electronics products Japan made, it exported them aggressively. This seriously dented the color TV industry in the United States, which in the 1970s accused its Eastern rival of price dumping. The feud ended in the Japanese agreeing to limit exports, but the country continued its charge by investing directly in the United States itself. Not content with taking existing pieces of equipment and making them better, Japan also broke new ground by pioneering video cassette recorders, camcorders and CD players. The country was also outsourcing before most people had even heard the term, retaining production of the most hi-tech items and farming out the not-so-hi-tech manufacturing to places like Taiwan. Most shrewdly, while the Japanese market has been phenomenally successful in getting its merchandise into living rooms, offices and garages abroad, imports from the outside have been allowed much slower progress in Japan. And typically for Japan, it was aesthetic rather than business concerns that were in part responsible:

foreign cars made headway as a result of the increasingly affluent public developing more of an interest in European design.

The constant upward economic trends in Japan did, however, falter in the early 1990s. With the Japanese economy's heavy reliance on exports creating a strong yen, Japanese industry changed its focus to large-scale investing in land and stocks. Meanwhile, Japanese consumers continued to spend on consumer goods. At the end of the 1980s and early '90s, the so-called "bubble economy" finally burst. Economic growth slowed, corporate profits fell and companies and families alike had to tighten their belts. Though low by Western standards, Japan's highest unemployment rate of nearly five percent in the mid-to-late 1990s forced many to reconsider the long-standing principle of a job for life.

Left: The yen is one of the world's major currencies.

Below: Rules of etiquette are strictly observed in Japanese business culture.

So what is the secret of this super-efficient market? How does Japanese business work? Given the stock images of Japanese employees, it is easy to imagine how consistency is achieved. We picture rows of similarly attired employees, arriving at work early, leaving for home late, spending all their lives in the employ of one company. But while this may be something of an exaggeration, the work culture does lack the individualism characteristic of Western capitalist societies. Here it is the group, not the individual, that is number one. Consensus rather than conflict is the norm. Employees enjoy fitting in and identifying with their firm, which keeps company loyalty strong. Japanese take a long-term view of things. Akio Morita, who co-founded Sony, summed it up, telling an American audience, "We are focusing on business ten years in advance, while you seem to be concerned only with profits ten minutes from now. At that rate, you may well never be able to compete with us." The country's values have been shaped by Shinto, Buddhism, and Confucianism, and hard work and attention to detail are prized in the workplace.

For Western business visitors, Japanese business culture includes a great many customs and practices which may be surprising or difficult to understand. While businesspeople used to dealing with Westerners will offer a handshake as a greeting, it is still far more common for Japanese to greet one another by bowing. There is also a great deal of etiquette attached to the exchanging of business cards. It is considered good manners to present your business card at a first meeting, and to accept a card (called *meishi* in Japanese) with both hands and to place it carefully in a case or top jacket pocket—this shows respect for the person who has handed you their card.

For Japanese employees, even to get into the workplace—or, at least, into a prestigious workplace—is a challenge, resulting in the kind of hothouse atmosphere and pressured studying for which Asia has become known. The top companies

choose their recruits from the top universities, which means the pressure is on from a young age. Companies like to get hold of their workers young and mold them in the company image. The traditional practice was that once in, you are likely in for life. Flitting between jobs and careers has not traditionally been the Japanese way. Employees get plenty of benefits, but fast-track advancement is not likely to be one of them. Seniority trumps individual talent, and workers who joined a firm at the same time typically find their promotion and salary increases occur at the same rate. To do otherwise would be to jeopardize the harmony that is too crucial to the efficient running of the organization.

The subjugation of the self, long hours, avoidance of conflict to the point of not venturing to contradict a superior, and slow progression regardless of individual merit take their toll on the Japanese worker, who lets off steam at the end-of-year work party and in the after-work socializing that has taken rates of alcoholism to worrying levels. *Karoshi*, or death from overwork, is a peculiarly Japanese phenomenon, and work is often a factor in stress-related suicide. Whether its principles are benevolent or appropriate for the 21st century can be argued. But what the Japanese work culture has achieved in terms of world dominance, excellence and innovation is beyond doubt.

Above: Bright lights, big city: an archetypal vision of modern Japan.

Left: The supremacy of Japanese industry has left a huge imprint on the country's urban architecture.

Isolated, exotic and mysterious, the land of the rising sun has fascinated the outsider for centuries. It has retained the traditions and values that it held dear in ancient times—and yet it is responsible for some of the most modern innovations. It deliberately cut itself off from external influences—and yet its top companies have aggressively conquered the world. It still reveres Buddhist doctrine and celebrates Shinto festivals—and yet it is decidedly secular. The bright lights and mad, bewildering rush of Tokyo—against the contemplative serenity of a Japanese garden. The dignity of the samurai and mentor—against the silliness of Tamagotchi. Japan is truly a land of contrasts.

It is also a land of extremes. The highest life expectancy. The lowest birth rate. The most forward-thinking corporations. And its modern-day accomplishments were all achieved from the ashes of ignominy and defeat during World War II. From the devastation of Hiroshima and Nagasaki, the humiliation of a proud state under foreign occupation, to world-beating technology and the elevation of its style around the world, in culture, art, sports, and food, the island nation underwent an incredible revolution.

We know Japan—and we do not know it. While its iconic images—the samurai, the geisha, the kamikaze pilot, the refined tea ceremony, the deafening neon buzz of Tokyo—are familiar to us, its philosophy, traditions, and history will remain ever remote. But perhaps Japan does not even know itself. Its self-imposed isolation has been ended by a Western incursion. Tragedy, suffering, and threat—World War II, the suicide cult, death from overwork, the low birth rate—have given the country pause. It has had to question the values that have been passed down and ingrained over centuries. Caught between West and East, there are fundamental choices to make. Where now for Japan?

Left: Japan continues on its forward-looking path.

Right: The Nisshoki, or sun flag, symbol of a land caught between tradition and modernity.

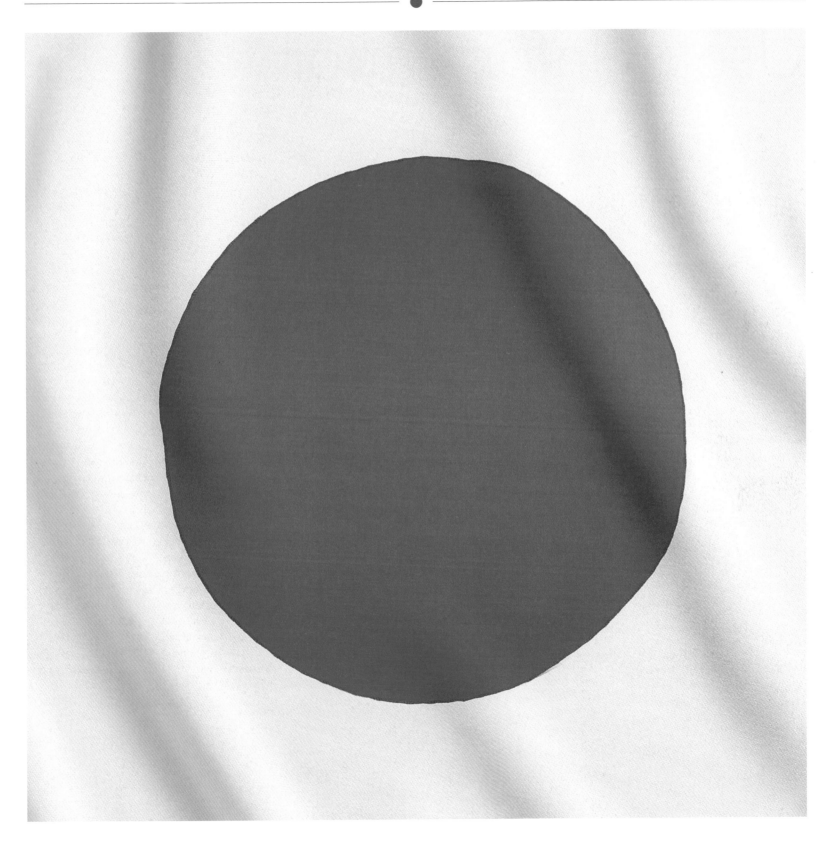

Useful Information

Japan National Tourist Organization

www.japantravelinfo.com/
New York office:
1 Rockefeller Plaza, Suite 1250
New York, NY 10020
Tel (212) 757-5640
Fax (212) 307-6754
visitjapan@jntonyc.org
Los Angeles office:
515 South Figueroa Street., Suite 1470
Los Angeles, CA 90071
Tel (213) 623-1952
Fax (213) 623-6301
info@jnto-lax.org

The Japan Foundation

www.jflalc.org/
New York Office:
152 West 57th Street, 17F
New York, NY 10019
Tel (212) 489-0299
Fax (212) 489-0409
Los Angeles Office:
333 South Grand Avenue, Suite 2250
Los Angeles, CA, 90071
Tel (213) 621-2267
Fax (213) 621-2590
Specialist organization for international cultural
exchange with Japan.

Asia Society

www.asiasociety.org
Selective annotated bibliography of English-language
publications on Japanese art, including armor, folk art,
and gardens.

Imperial Household Agency official homepage

www.kunaicho.go.jp/eindex.html
An introduction to the duties and public activities
of the members of Japan's Imperial Family, including
genealogy, personal history, traditional culture, and
public events.

Japan Association for Cultural Exchange

www.acejapan.or.jp/index.html
Information on Japanese culture and society from
ACE Japan, which develops cultural programs in
collaboration with the Japan Foundation and other
related organizations.

Japan Times

www.japantimes.co.jp
The electronic edition of Japan's leading English-
language newspaper.

NHK English

www.nhk.or.jp/english/
The English-language website of NHK, Japan's national
TV and radio broadcaster. The site includes news and
other video clips as well as a series of audio lessons
for learners of Japanese.

Japan Links / Web Japan

web-japan.org/links/culture/index.html
Contact information for cultural organizations,
including museums and galleries, music, hobbies, art,
arts and entertainment, sports, and religion.

Japan Focus

http://japanfocus.org
Writings about Japan, Japan in Asia and the world, as
well as Japanese and international perspectives on
contemporary politics, economics and society.

Japan Guide

www.japan-guide.com
First-hand information on traveling and living in Japan.

Japanese American National Museum

www.janm.org/
369 East First Street
Los Angeles, California 90012
Tel (213) 625-0414
Fax (213) 625-1770
The only museum in the United States dedicated
to sharing the experience of Americans of Japanese
ancestry.

National Theater of Japan

www.ntj.jac.go.jp
Includes the introduction, history and description of
traditional Japanese performing arts.

Japan Origami Academic Society

www.origami.gr.jp

Features a gallery of images of origami, magazine articles, links to other origami sites, and information on origami artists.

Tea Ceremony

www.teahyakka.com

A bilingual site with a history and description of the tea ceremony, information on tea classes offered outside Japan, links, and a message board.

Bonsai Site

www.bonsaisite.com

Comprehensive site with tips, history, and pointers to further sources of information.

All Martial Arts

History, description, and equipment for the main martial arts.

www.allmartialarts.com

Samurai Archives

www.samurai-archives.com

Historical, cultural, and personal description of the samurai phenomenon.

Index